M000104059

UNSTOPPABLE

Leverage Life Setbacks
to Build Resilience for Success

Elite Foundation® Publisher

Ft. Lauderdale, Florida

Inspired Stories of Real People with
Unconquerable Will to Thrive and Be Alive

Published by Elite Foundation®, Fort Lauderdale, Florida

Book Cover: Jesus Cordero
Editorial Review: Elite Literary Team
Elite Foundation® is a registered trademark
Printed in the United States of America.

ISBN: 978-1-7320778-6-7

This publication is designed to provide accurate and authoritative information regarding the subject matter covered. It is sold with the understanding that the publisher is not engaged in rendering legal, accounting, clinical or other professional advice. If legal advice or other expert assistance is required, the services of a competent professional should be sought. The opinions expressed by the authors in this book are not endorsed by Elite Foundation and are the sole responsibility of the author rendering the opinion.

Most Elite Foundation® titles are available in bulk purchases for sales promotions, premiums, fundraising, and educational use. Special versions or book excerpts can also be created on direct request for specific needs aligned with Elite Foundation®

For more information, please write:

Elite Foundation® Publisher

2003 West Cypress Creek Road, Suite 103, Ft. Lauderdale, Florida 33369

Or email: ElitePublisher@EliteFundsFreedom.org

Visit us online: www.EliteFundsFreedom.org/book_program

Elite Foundation is a 501(c)(3) nonprofit organization that offers Indie publishing services through the Foundation's eAcademy. When you invest in yourself, you Fund Freedom. Royalties from all our goods and services support scholarships/grants and the work done with victims and survivors of human exploitation and trafficking. Elite Foundation's vision is powered by people coming together to bring an end to human exploitation and trafficking by co-creating a future for every survivor.

UNSTOPPABLE

" We may encounter many defeats, but we must never be

defeated."

~Maya Angelou

The depiction of the humanity found within the pages of this artistic process work, is no less than an authentic reflection of the many threads found within a system of intricate experiences, that when weaved together, create pathways. Pathways predicated upon knowledge transpired through generational learning, but uniquely experienced by each human being at different moments in time.

Each contribution has significance, valued by those either who share in the experience or by those who are spectators seeking to emulate or to avoid the pain. As you embark upon the collective consciousness shared in Unstoppable, navigate the experience totally present in the moment. Use caution not to become immersed, unless it serves. There is rarity of transparency within the pages of the text; but also, reflection of some of the least desirable attributes and behaviors that man can inflict upon itself.

Transcend the obvious, in order to fully appreciate what you are supposed to learn, now.

The intent of our work, whether it be perceived from the context of self, work or humanity, is to ignite and engage, in order to affect the actualization of personal and community transformation through actionable faith, hope and unconditional love.

Unstoppable, is the third installment in a world class international bestselling series of books created to inspire others through stories of real people, who despite or in some cases because of circumstance, make choices that edify the very best of what we all seek and, in the process, build the skills needed for a successful life of balance and wholeness.

Through this text you will learn of the importance of building the psychological skill of resilience. And further that resilience is crucial to avoid the potentially debilitating effects of stress/negative energy associated with life difficulties and trauma. Through the strategies, tools, and knowledge shared we equip others to affect change. There are beneficial attributes associated with resiliency, as it relates to experiencing improved learning and achievement, lowered absences from responsibilities due to sickness, reduced use of risk-taking behaviors such as excessive drinking, smoking or use of drugs, increased involvement in community and family activities and a lower rate of mortality and increased physical health.

Elite Authors are disruptors, who seek excellence in pursuit of the audience of one. Influencers and Thought Leaders, who value the importance of compassion, generosity and integrity, while employing courage from within, to invest in others. Socially-conscious individuals, who have achieved in life and business, but not without the realizations that result from living. It is these very unique, but collective experiences that contribute to what is known about the power of resilience and its impact on becoming an unstoppable Warrior for Change.

> "Our lives begin to end the day that we become silent about the things that matter."
>
> ~Martin Luther King, Jr.

Dr. Jessica Vera, Ph.D.
Award Winning Multiple Bestseller
Elite Foundation

CONTENT

vi

PART I

The Power of Leverage:

Activate Internal

Resources

Ants, Pain and Purpose

Author: Dede Lomenick

When I was younger, I was fascinated by ants. Maybe it was because I was so close to the ground! They were so organized and industrious! Talk about being on a mission! Those tiny critters were 100% missional! They all had a job to do and they were going to work until they finished it!! Every ant was totally focused. Until. Until I would drag my finger through their orderly line. When my finger cut through the line, I disrupted their system and they lost their connection. Chaos ensued. What was once a picture of uniformity and progress turned into mass confusion. And as the confusion grew, the mission gave way to panic.

Life has a funny way of seeking to disrupt our organized systems. There have been times that I was sure that I was on a mission from God and it felt like the divine hand from on high dragged His finger through my orderly world and, like the ants, chaos ensued. Oh boy - chaos most definitely ensued. I have been left feeling confused and devastated - wondering how I ended up in such a broken mess. Ever feel like that?

My husband and I have three incredible daughters and back when they were much younger, I started having a pain that wouldn't't go away on my left side. It got to the point where I finally went to the doctor who sent me to another doctor. Many appointments later I ended up in surgery and was misdiagnosed.

That began a 9-year, 5 surgery odysseys of chronic, debilitating pain. I was in bed almost all the time for weeks at a time. There is so much pain and suffering packed into the above sentence. It would be impossible for me to adequately express how arduous and depressing it was.

Chronic pain does a number on you. It debilitates your body and your mind. For me, it completely altered the mission that I thought I had for my life. I thought I was right where God wanted me to be - married to a pastor, raising my kids, involved in ministry and loving it. A pastor's wife for crying out loud! How much more missional could I be? My life was one giant mission and this major hiccup was not on mission. At least not on my mission. Plus, it was awful. And, to be honest, it was embarrassing. My sweet spot had been helping other people - definitely NOT being the one that needed help all the time. It was humiliating to be the one that was sick all the time, the one who was always asking for rides for her kids, the one who couldn't't come to events or even show up to church most weeks (usually pastor's wives should actually go to church once in a while).

There were times where the pain was so intense, I would lay in bed and sob. I would cry out to God and beg for relief. I spent hours listening to the Bible online trying to keep my mind occupied. During this season, I fell in love with the book of Psalms. The guy that wrote most of the psalms, David, was usually a hot mess and all over the map emotionally. I could TOTALLY relate to that! So, one day as I was doing my sobbing/writhing in pain/hot mess routine in my bed the Bible narrator read this verse: "On my bed I remember you; I think of you through the watches of the night" (Psalm 63:6 NIV). Hmmmmmm - what did those sixteen words mean for me? Was it possible to somehow serve God from my bed?

Pain - emotional or physical makes us change our priorities completely. C.S. Lewis puts it like this, "Pain insists upon being attended to. God whispers to us in our pleasures, speaks in our conscience, but shouts in our pains. It is his megaphone to rouse a deaf world." That is the TRUTH right there! It cannot and will not be ignored no matter how hard we try. We sure do try to ignore it, though don't we?

When we are in intense pain, we seek to find ways to make the pain stop. If that does not work, we try to distract ourselves from it. But what if - what if. . . we allowed ourselves to feel the pain instead of trying to escape from it? What if we started finding ways to walk through the pain whether it's physical, emotional or spiritual? Is it possible that pain could actually be our ally instead of our enemy? I was determined to find out.

When my girls were little, I loved reading them the book called We're Going on a Bear Hunt by Michael Rosen. We read it over and over. There was a phrase repeated throughout the book that went like this:

"We're going on a bear hunt.

We're going to catch a big one.

What a beautiful day!

We're not scared.

(Insert obstacle here)

We can't go over it.

We can't go under it.

Oh no!

We've got to go through it!"

What if we went through the pain rather than trying to avoid it? What if we allowed ourselves to feel it without trying to run from it or numb it or push it down? How would that change things?

In the Bible there's this crazy story about a guy named Jacob wrestling with an angel. Weird right? So, let me give you a little backstory. Jacob was a total jerk. Jacob's name meant to assail or overreach. He was trouble from the time he was born! His twin brother was named Esau and when their mom gave birth, Jacob was born holding onto his brother's heel (Genesis 25). Not a great first impression. He came out of the womb fighting to be first and that tendency never left him. Jacob spent his life scrambling to be on top. He wanted to have the highest position the most stuff - whatever it took. He was so worried about "having it all" that he lied to become heir to his father's estate. A right that was typically reserved

5

for the first born. Now he had made an enemy of his own twin brother. And that twin brother was out for blood.

So, Jacob ran - no sprinted - for his life. Yup. He was a liar, a deceiver and a coward. He knew that his brother was coming after him to kill him, so he had his servant spy on his brother and give him a full report. The report was bad news. His brother was coming and bringing 400 men with him. Maybe now Jacob would get his act together and go face his consequences. NOPE. "Then Jacob was greatly afraid and distressed. He divided the people who were with him, and the flocks and herds and camels, into two camps, thinking, 'If Esau comes to the one camp and attacks it, then the camp that is left will escape'" (Genesis 32:7-8). The nerve of this guy!! He decided that it would be better to risk the lives of half of his family, people and animals rather than doing the right thing.

Still nervous about his impending doom, Jacob "prays". He does not pray, he "prays". His main objective was not to set things right. Jacob's goal was to shoot up an emergency "prayer flare" and pray that God would somehow spare him from the consequences he deserved. I can totally relate to that move. I've done that way more than I care to admit. When things seem under control, I'm cool, calm and collected. But the second that trouble starts I finally figure out that maybe it's time to actually reach out for some divine intervention. But only as a last resort.

Maybe dividing everyone into two camps and praying wasn't quite enough. Jacob sure didn't think it was. He decided that, just to be extra safe, he would give his brother a present. That should fix everything. Rather than admit what you've done, just give them a gift. UGH! I've done this too! See, the thing is, I see myself all through this story and it isn't pretty. Genesis 32:20-21 says "For he (Jacob) thought, 'I may appease him with the present that goes ahead of me, and afterward I shall see his face. Perhaps he will accept me;' So the present passed on ahead of him, and he himself stayed that night in the camp." Jacob sent the gift but was unwilling to send himself.

So far, the story seems pretty straight forward. Jacob does everything but the right thing and is hoping to squeak it out one more time. But then this happens - "And Jacob was left alone. And a man wrestled with him until the breaking of the day. When the man saw that he did not prevail against Jacob, he touched his hip socket, and Jacob's hip was put out of joint as he wrestled with him. Then he said, 'Let me go, for the day has broken.' But Jacob said, 'I will not let you go unless you bless me.' And he said to him, 'What is your name?' And he said, 'Jacob.' Then he said, 'Your name shall no longer be called Jacob, but Israel, for you have striven with God and with men, and have prevailed.' Then Jacob asked him, 'Please tell me your name.' But he said, 'Why is it that you ask my name?' And there he blessed him. So, Jacob called the name of the place Peniel, saying, 'For I have seen God face to face, and yet my life has been delivered.' The sun rose upon him as he passed Penuel, limping because of his hip" (Genesis 32:24-31).

Um, what just happened?

Let's recap:

*Jacob is a jerk.

*Jacob deceives his brother.

*Jacob runs away.

*Jacob "prays".

*Jacob's brother is coming after him to kill him.

*Jacob sends a servant to check out the situation.

Spy returns. Bad news. Brother is TICKED and has brought 400 of his closest friends to make a point.

*Jacob splits his camp in half and figures at least 50% of them will make it. (Too bad if you're in the wrong half.)

(Jacob gives a gift to his brother hoping that will smooth things over.

OK - so all of this is making sense to me. UNTIL THE GUY SHOWS UP and they go all World Wrestling Federation. Who was the man? What does it all mean? To be honest, I can't tell you exactly what it means. But I can tell you this, God knows that sometimes we are hard headed creatures and sometimes we need an object lesson to open our eyes. Jacob wrestling with this being/angel/God is a reminder that all of us wrestle with him in different ways.

Which brings me back to my bed. I spent countless hours begging God to get me out of the situation. I plead with Him to make the pain stop. Years went by. Nine long years. I wrestled and He would not relent. So, like Jacob, I said "I will not let you go unless you bless me. Come hell or high water, I will not let you go." And I didn't let go. Instead I asked God to show me more of Him and He began to reveal ways that I could care for others while flat on my back. And that is just what I did. I chose to go through the pain and seek God in the middle of the mess. Now I look back at that time with great fondness and gratitude.

But why would God allow my pain and why would he put Jacob's hip out of joint? It says that Jacob walked with a limp for the rest of his life. A permanent physical reminder of the wrestling match. Could that pain be a gift? "This was an evidence of a divine touch indeed, which wounded and healed at the same time." (Matthew Henry, Complete Bible Commentary). If we allow ourselves to go through whatever pain, we are in without trying to hide from it we gain profound clarity. Pain does realign our priorities.

For me, pain ended up changing my priorities in the most unimaginable ways. I became more honest with God, myself and other people. I quit trying so hard to look like I had it all together - because I didn't. Most days I couldn't pull myself together enough to stop crying. Seriously. I'm a "look on the bright side" kind of gal so this level of honesty and openness about the darkness within me was scary at first. Then I started to find out that I was still loved. I was loved by my family and friends just because they loved me. Imagine that! I didn't have to work so hard. In fact, I didn't have to work at all.

Pain taught me courage and gave me the ability to prioritize others over myself in the midst of it. When my pain was at its peak, I realized that the one thing that I could do no matter what was pray for people. And so, I did. I prayed and prayed and prayed. I texted encouragement and prayers to people. I asked for friends to share their burdens and I followed up with them. I had never prayed so much in my life. I had never prayed FOR OTHER PEOPLE AND NOT MYSELF so much in my life. Did my pain go away? Not for a very long time. But I was outside of myself and my mission became laser focused. And, for once, it wasn't laser focused on me.

Once I changed my perspective, it changed me. I became missional again. In fact, more missional than I had ever been. God hadn't knocked me off of my mission He redirected and expanded my mission. There is a verse that I love and have held onto since then, "to comfort all who mourn, and provide for those who grieve —to bestow on them a crown of beauty instead of ashes."(Isaiah 61:2-3 NIV) I have always loved the idea of a crown of glory. I mean, a crown! Awesome, right? But one day I read that verse and realized that the ashes come before the crown. There are always ashes.

It is up to us whether we accept the ashes and learn from them or we resist that part and keep trying to fast-forward to the crown. Our ability to accept our seasons of ashes can be amazing or amazingly hard.

"Of one thing I am perfectly sure: God's story never ends with ashes." (Elisabeth Elliot).

About Dede Lomenick

Dede Lomenick is a joyful yet perpetually tired pastor's wife and mama to three amazing girls - ages 22, 18 and 16. (And yes, having three girls at those ages is as expensive as it sounds. Just the personal care products alone....)

She loves speaking and performing stand-up comedy and has a passionate desire to see people live life to the fullest. She writes original comedy material and song parodies about her life, family and mostly about the ridiculous situations she finds herself in! Dede has been speaking, singing and entertaining in one form or another for over 25 years. She also loves to write about herself in the third person which is weird but not harmful most of the time.

Dede is the founder of Unleashed - an event designed to help women to discover and leverage their gifts to impact the world around them. She also created an original comedy event in South Florida known as the Divine MOMedy featuring stand-up comedy, song parodies and her all girl band The Raging Hormones. The Divine MOMedy just celebrated its third birthday and has gained a great following.

To contact Dede Lomenick:

dede.lomenick@gmail.com (email)

or visit

www.dedelomenick.com (website)

The Leap.

By: Anastasia Pitanova

An authentic story of how to use your darkest moments in life to create a momentum of growth, happiness and joy.

Each of us has a story to tell and might arrive at a point in life when it becomes so big, it is time to release it with transparency.

I have questioned internally about how to share the story of my life for a long time. But now I feel it's important to be authentic and shows through my journey that anything is possible to those who choose the path of their heart and stayed loyal to their dreams no matter what setbacks they have in life.

Rise above your circumstances. Dream Big.

I spent my childhood in a small Russian village where my family moved from Kazakhstan after the Soviet Union collapsed. The population of this little town was approximately 3000 people, less than the number of students in some high schools today. At that time, my country was facing a deep depression. Because of the monetary reform and some other political factors, in a short few months, many families, including ours, lost everything.

Suddenly, we went from being an upper-middle-class to becoming very poor and found ourselves in a financial crisis we weren't ready for.

Most of what we knew stopped existing in a blink of an eye. The economy of the country collapsed, and it affected all areas of our lives: from access to international travels to simple access to cloth, food, and oftentimes hot water. It was shocking!

As a result, during my childhood we didn't have much. Often had no money for a new pair of shoes, we lived very frugally trying to make the end needs.

Our parents did all they possibly could to provide and to break through their circumstances to give us the best life possible. Even though we didn't have some of the material blessings and lived in a very limited environment, we, as the family always found time to dream and have fun together.

You see, dreaming and one's imagination cannot be taken away and it's something that is always available, no matter what the circumstances are.

At a very early age, I was exposed to amazing literature from classics to new age, esoteric to religious reads, personal development, etc. I was reading everything I possibly could, as it was my escape from the reality, I was in.

I did very well at school, due to the fact that I kept myself busy with my studies and activities. I was hungry for life in all its forms just because I saw that there was something bigger out there than what we had in front of us at the time.

Some of my first spiritual teachers were: Dr. Wayne Dyer, Deepak Chopra, and Louise Hay, Brian Tracy, Napoleon Hill. I was amazed by their work. These readings led me to have dreams of living a rich, impactful life and since I was 12 years old, I knew that my life would be different. I knew that my vision of the future did not belong within the confines of my childhood reality.

During my 3rd year in University, the opportunity to leave the country and continue studying in the United States presented itself. My decision was made instantly. There were no questions or doubt, no second-guessing. I knew that this was what I needed to do. I felt fully confident and certain. That was one of the first big shifts that took place in my life.

From a young woman to become a completely grown adult, who feels whole within, I had to have the freedom to experience, to grow, to explore, in the process of discovery.

I like the story of the Buddha, who shares that he had to escape from his royal family in order to find the path to enlightenment. He did not know what was going to happen. All he knew was that there was a higher calling and it required him to get out of his comfort zone and explore.

I believe this was also part of my journey of how I came in the United States. Very naive, full of ambition and goals, absolutely not grounded. I have made many mistakes and at the same time, I achieved some very exciting results. But most importantly, what I am grateful for is that my experiences in finding myself led me to wholeness, once I broke through trauma, healing and was reborn into a woman, who can take unshakable steps and lead others. It did not happen overnight, in my journey it took more than a decade, but every second and each lesson was worth it.

Failure and Breakthrough.

You are not your mistakes and in fact, there are no mistakes in life, only experience. I believe, we always do our best on a level that we are at. It might seem like a terrible failure sometimes and even feels like that too, but trust me, it all will pass, and life will be bright again.

I met my ex-husband the same year I arrived in the United States. We got married way too early and way too immature. The euphoria of love and emotions took over the ability to make proper judgments and conclusions. We weren't ready to create a family, but we did. And it brought us to the life of so much stress and pressure so both of us stopped being ourselves. From the loving and supportive couple, we once were, we become disconnected and very cold towards each other. As new immigrants and young parents, we were facing a lot of financial and emotional challenges and we weren't ready for it.

The distance between us became so big and obvious, fighting and ignorance became our day after day reality.

On my fifth year of marriage, I was ready to leave but was holding on for the children, hoping that transformation of the relationship was possible. But the momentum of disrespect, distance, tears, and pain was too strong.

After almost 10 years of marriage, the day arrived that would forever change the trajectory of my life. There was no coming back from this point. I stood in front of the mirror and looked into my own eyes questioning:

What happened to me-young beautiful woman, who now was feeling lifeless and completely in denial of herself?

Often times suicidal, the only thing that kept me going was the love for my children.

But when did I lose my own desire to live?

Everything that I knew about my life was falling apart. I was facing a divorce, blaming myself for not being a good mother to my beautiful sons.

I often questioned: Being a mother and having a family was something I really wanted, isn't it?

And oftentimes I hated this part of my life. I had failed to build a career and was feeling like I would never be able to do what I wanted again. Taking care of the children seemed so difficult, exhausting and something that I really did not want to do at the time. I was ready to give up. I was carrying so much guilt and pain from even thinking this way. It was scary. I was crushing. But, all the while, smiling and being a good mother and a wife in front of others in public. I was covering up what was really going on in my life. I got to the point where it was so difficult to breathe and move forward.

What is wrong with me?

Why had I lost my identity?

It felt like I was jumping from the cliff of uncertainty and I wanted to let everything just disappear. I wanted to close my eyes and let the Universe wash away all my problems and hold me. From the young ambitious and powerful woman, who was creating her life on her own terms, I became a lifeless victim with no boundaries. I was miserable and sick of myself. It became overwhelming until it hit me, Enough!

I craved a change. I craved to bring back the one who was fearless, powerful, beautiful, loving and free. But the distance between the current me and HER felt unreachable.

Trust that everything in your life is in perfect order and at the right time. Trust the change and be ready to leap into the life that is waiting for you.

In the moment of our deepest confusion and trauma, we all need someone who will lift us up. It can be through training, a coach, good friends, community, starting a new exciting career and meeting new positive and uplifting people. But most importantly it requires our own work on our self-beliefs and self-image.

Right before the divorce, we moved from one state to another, where I didn't know anyone, and I realized that it's an amazing opportunity to rebuild everything from scratch. I started a new career, exposed myself to transformational trainings and started looking for new connections with people I wanted to become. Slowly, day by day, everything started to shift. It felt like the skin I have burned started to heal and new skin was appearing beautifully. I began to discover who I was again. But it wasn't an overnight process.

I started simply by being patient with myself and letting all feelings come into my consciousness. You see, the biggest misconception of our times is that we all are looking for Good experience. Positive thinking, affirmations, and search for fulfillment become our obsession. We automatically separate the negative and painful moments like it doesn't have the permission to have existed. But we are here not only to feel good but simply to feel. Feel everything, feel with every cell of our body. And this is what I did.

I was still scared but let myself dive deeply into love, sadness, misery, fear. I let myself stay in bed and be not responsible, just let myself fully BE and trust that it is ok to let everything fall apart. It was okay not to have the ground under my feet, and it was absolutely okay to not know what is next.

My mind was affected with false beliefs of not being worthy and enough for success and happiness I was craving, I couldn't trust it.

The only choice that was able to lead me to a transformation, is to follow my heart again, let go of control and expectations of how my life should look like and just follow my inner instincts. Do everything that felt light and exciting, let myself be joyful and free.

Very gradually I started hearing my own voice. First, it was a whisper, then it became louder, then I wasn't able to hear anything else but it. I had no choice but surrender.

Your true passion is where you connect to your Soul. Find it and be reborn there.

A desire to paint was born one evening. It started with the light feeling of taking the brush and to start exploring. It grew day after day, and I came to the point where it became bigger than me. It started moving me toward the future I have never imagined and opened opportunities I haven't dreamed of.

It's been exactly 2 years and a half from the moment I created my first artwork. Since then I completed over 60 paintings and I have sold most of them. I have participated in numerous art shows and had my first solo exhibition. All this happened with me doing really nothing but diving into my gift and becoming attuned to the energy that flows through me and manifests itself in my paintings.

Each of the art pieces shows the biggest breakthroughs: healing moments, moments of deepest pain and happiness, lessons I have learned.

One of my first work "Raising Phoenix" is a representation of freedom of the human spirit and inner power that we all hold within. At the moment of creating that piece, I felt that transformation is unavoidable and all I needed to do is to trust my own wings and remember how to fly again.

Because my heart and living in harmony with my inner truth became my priority, the transformation happened in all areas of life. In a short few years of complete surrender and trust, my life unfolded into a beautiful story. The right people showed up at the right time. Opportunities just flowed organically, time and possibilities appear magically. I was able to establish a successful career as a Realtor and an artist, to be a philanthropist and very present mother to my growing children. Showing them authentically how to forgive, be flexible, how to be yourself, I teach them the primary lesson of following their dreams and creating happiness for themselves, where later they can invite others to join.

Each of us has wings and that creative space, where connection to the soul is so strong and clear that all answers are instant and powerful. And I don't know what that space looks like for you specifically. Maybe you have always wanted to paint, play an instrument, maybe you always dreamed of being a comedian, no matter what it is, I guarantee, when you surrender to your brightest talent, your life will never be the same. You will become an Alchemist of your own reality. Will you have loss? Yes, of course!

Some of my closest friends turned away at the darkest moments. I wasn't able to understand why, but it wasn't important anymore. I had ME back and, I was able to build a community of incredible women, leaders, visionaries, with whom we can create day after day, and build a foundation of support for others. Often times I am not able to believe that this is where my life is shifting now.

But what I know for sure is that everything is possible! Everything is, as long as we become an instrument for the Universe and surrender to its music!

No matter what you are facing now, no matter how difficult it is, I want to let you know that it will pass, and another moment will come. Just like the sun rises every morning. Life will happen again and again, and it will be difficult not only once. And sometimes it will feel like it's over, but you are still alive, and it means you need to find a way to keep going.

"Be a process, not a result, and you will see how unlimited you truly are"

About Anastasia Pitanova

 Mother, Artist, Entrepreneur, Author, Anastasia believes that we all have unlimited potential and can have it all!

Originally from Russia, she always had a dream to impact others' lives. Being an entrepreneur all her life, Anastasia had very a deep passion for discovering human potential, and what others can do to live beautiful, vibrant lives. Since moving to United States in 2005, Anastasia has been on her journey of self-discovery.

With more than a decade of formal study and exploring different teachings and spiritual practices, she has learned - there is no magical pill for success, there is no right or wrong circumstances, there is no luck. Everyone has an unlimited potential for creating life by their own design. No matter what you are struggling with finances, relationships, harmony, or health success begins with strong discipline, the right habits and every day rituals. It is a conscious choice to take responsibility to develop a prosperous Mindset and to be committed to your dreams.

Anastasia has completed numerous leadership and transformational trainings, including training with Tony Robbins, Gratitude Training, Landmark Forum and others. She is a creator of several transformational programs using art therapy, and her aspiration is to bring them to the community, specifically to help young children and teenagers, who find themselves in the foster care system and survivors.

"My vision is a world full of shining eyes of happiness, self-expression, confidence and free human beings, where everything is possible and it's safe to be yourself"

To connect with Anastasia Pitanova: website: artofanastasiapitanova.com

Facebook.com/sia.nova.art

https://www.facebook.com/SiaNovaArt/

Instagram: sia.nova.art

Wired for Rescue

Finding Identity and Purpose in Life's imperfection

By: Mary Jane Piedra

Diving deep into the banks of my memory, I remember the first time I felt, "The Tug." I can still see her little light brown face, framed by shiny black curls, with big streaming tears running down her cheeks, as her little chest heaved up and down, trying to squeeze out all her inner grief. There, standing in front of my first-grade class, was a new girl. My teacher tried so hard to comfort her, but in a language she could not understand. There it was, that tug, that feeling that wanted to make my body jump out of my chair and walk over to her to embrace and comfort her- Her anguish, unsettled my little world. Suddenly, the teacher looked up and called my name to come over and say hello! It was as if the tug was released, and I was free to do what I longed for, which was to ease her suffering.

Since that day, this tug has continued to surface throughout my life. It has impacted me in both positive and negative ways. It has been given many names- from heroic to enabling and even crazy. It has been however, what I believe to be foundational in developing and transforming me from the inside out.

The tug has caused me to elevate to new heights of risk and reward, but also taken me to a place of retreat, self-evaluation, and healing. It is a huge part of my life story and how I am wired. It has led me and taught me about my identity and purpose. It has also led

25

me to a deeper connection to the One who designed me, knowing exactly how He would use it.

Flashback to 1999, there I am a career driven, pencil skirt wearing, divorced woman and mother of two teenaged girls. When it came to advancing my career quickly; the tug, had served me well. I was sensitive and efficient in achieving the desires and goals of my superiors and clients, as Director of Sales for a successful boutique hotel in Miami.

In my personal life there was a contrast however, where the tug led me into a few relationships with nice, yet emotionally wounded men. I would date these men, nurture them back to being confident, only to be dumped a few months later. The time and energy spent in these relationships needless to say had also derailed other more important relationships and areas in my life.

For the most part, I grew up in a non-religious home. God was only mentioned in the guise of an enforcer when my behavior fell short of my parent's expectations. I don't recall hearing that He loved me and had a good and special plan for my life. Thankfully that would change. Sometime later a friend invited me to their church, which wasn't like other churches I had visited. This one was in a warehouse building. As I entered, I remember walking toward a light-filled stage packed with a huge and diverse choir. The music was joyful and lively. People were happily singing and raising their arms as if they were in a concert.

My level of discomfort shot through the roof, however there it was again, that little tug just drawing me closer to the front. I probably looked like a deer in the headlights, but once I began to listen to the pastor's message, I heard how much God loved me; how He created me for good things and had paid for all my mistakes. Not only my mistakes, but that of the whole worlds. I was taken aback. Why hadn't anyone ever told me this? Maybe they did, but I just didn't get it. Well, I got it then, and as I left the church looking the same, somehow, I knew everything was different. It was like the Jesus I had gazed upon the cross for so many years, stepped down and wrapped his loving arms around me, and was now walking alongside me. He knew everything about me and still loved me and I could now trust him. So that day, I gave Him all of me, including the tug.

A few months after my surrender experience, I had a business trip with my boss to New York City. He was a strong leader, and a mentor to me as well as to the staff of the hotel. He was analytical and in charge. Our relationship had always been very professional, yet somehow friendly. Little did I know our relationship would drastically change on this trip, and that five short months later, we would be married! Yes, it was fast, and most would say crazy, but in this instance, the tug took over. Logically speaking, our relationship based on our opposing personalities, could never work.

Needless to say, our first year of marriage was challenging. Our different views of the world merged with my two teenaged daughters, his diabetic dog and a rabbit we were all allergic to named Mrs. Breeze. Much to my surprise, this ambitious career woman decided then that it was best to stay home throughout this messy process. A process that if not for supernatural intervention, would have ended in disaster. Through all the growing pains, we slowly started becoming a family and soon after, my husband's job took us to New Orleans. We were away from family and friends, which brought new challenges, but thankfully forced us to be much closer. We even added a new baby girl and another pup which made all of us officially bonded.

As for "the tug", looking back, it was pretty dormant at that time, or maybe it was just waiting for the craziness that came next. After two years in New Orleans, my husband's next job took us to the Bahamas.

All of us went with the exception of my then college-aged daughter, who returned to Miami.

Life for me in the Bahamas was an easy adjustment. The laid-back lifestyle suited my personality. I enjoyed a lovely apartment within the resort, as well as housekeeping services and eight restaurants to please a variety of cravings. I made good friends who like me, were expatriated due to their husbands' jobs. We all had young children and for the most part, spent our days at the beach and poolside playdates which culminated into the traditional island's 6 o'clock wine time. Yes, life was close to a paradise that would soon come to an end.

I remember the day like it was yesterday. The island was on an evacuation warning due to a hurricane watch for an approaching direct hit by Frances, a category 4 storm. My husband begged me to take the kids and leave along with all my friends and hotel guests who were now boarding company charter flights, but I refused. He stormed out of the room calling me irresponsible. Yes, the tug was holding me back from leaving. Crying, I continued to pack our valuables and essentials to move up to a higher floor due to the anticipated storm surge. That night before the storm, as my husband prepared the hotel, I sat together with my two girls, my dogs and the tug, yet, an overwhelming sense of peace surrounded me. I knew it was from my Savior.

Hurricane Frances must have loved our island. She hovered over us with her category 3 winds and rain for three days. Our island was completely devastated. We had no power, no communication, and our airport was flooded and closed. What we did have was the harsh reality that it would be a while before any help came. Soon, along with a select group of our hotel staff, I found myself passing out supplies and food in a nearby village where many of our employees lived. My heart broke as I saw how little everyone had left. Then, I saw him- A beautiful dark-skinned young man. He was leaning up against a car holding a tiny three-week old infant over his shoulder. He was silently looking down as tears rolled down his face. His wife had left the island, and him and their two children.

All of a sudden, there it was, "the tug", so strong- that I ran over to him and without thinking, told him that although I didn't know how, I would find a way to help his baby which was now only days away from no formula, diapers or water, and without government aid coming any time soon. That night, I couldn't eat or sleep. My husband was working tirelessly to get help for the island as I lay in bed staring at my 18-month old daughter wearing nothing but a diaper due to the intense humidity and heat. All I could think about was the baby, somewhere in the dark and his poor young father.

The next day, I went back accompanied by hotel security staff my husband insisted come with me. Thankfully, I had managed to find diapers in our housekeeping department along with towels and bottles of water. I also brought some of my daughter's formula I had stocked up on. Sadly, when I got there, he was nowhere to be found. However, when some of the other mothers saw my supplies, they swarmed around my SUV to the point that security had to cover me and take us away. As we drove off, there they were, more babies, not the one I was looking for, but oh so many more. All of them being held by desperate teary faces. I wanted to stop the car and give them what we had, but security wouldn't allow me. I cried uncontrollably as one them patted me and said: "There's not much you can do Mrs. Amaury", but the tug insisted and won!

After another sleepless night, I snuck my husband's satellite phone from his night table, and from my balcony, I prayed and asked God to tell me who to call and what to do. I called my island friends who were on the mainland all scattered in different areas. I daringly called my husband's VP at the corporate office, and even called a realtor whose card had mysteriously fallen onto the floor and whom I had barely met when I first came to the island. I don't know what I told them, but two days later, there was a small army forming at the front of my hotel asking for me. Merchants started to open their stores to give me baby supplies, as money came in from the States through corporate planes that my husband's VP had sent. Over fifty hotels within the chain had collected money to send to the babies; even some plastic jugs of water were filled with money! It was then that the Bahama Babies Relief Fund was born. As my friends returned to the island, they joined the effort. Never did I imagine that prayer and a few desperate phone calls could ignite so much love and support. It was as if God heard my despair and miraculously formed this army, that during the island's six-month recovery period, provided diapers, formula and cereal to over 160 babies in need.

Newspapers and news radio hailed me as some sort of hero, but I knew who the real hero was. It was Him, the One who had wired me, and now I understood that not only had He wired me, but that He had wired me for rescue. Soon after, a promotion for my husband took us back home to South Florida. Our baby was now two and a half, and our middle daughter started her senior year of high school. We began noticing that our oldest daughter who had stayed behind while we were away, was very different and soon discovered it had to do with drugs- The kind few people ever recover from.

There I was, a so-called hero, on my knees with my face buried in the sofa trying to muffle out the sound of my loud cries. What kind of mother was I? How could I have left her behind? I was overcome by grief and remorse. Then suddenly this still small voice whispered in my overwhelmed heart: "That's enough! Now, are you ready for me to fix this?" It was so real that it immediately halted my episode of fear and guided me over to the Yellow Pages (pre-Google times) and there it was: "Faith Farm Ministries" It was there that my daughter agreed to live for the next six months. As I visited her and began to see what God was doing to heal her, I also started to discover things in me that I was not aware of. I was carrying things like unforgiveness, anger, shame and grief. As my daughter was being cared for, I was also able to retreat and not be the rescuer but allow myself to be rescued this time.

As my eldest returned to a fully functional healthy life, I came home one day to find my 19-year old daughter weeping over her laptop, seeking help. She was pregnant. Thankfully because of everything God had shown me, the tug this time without hesitation, gave me the right words to ease her fears and encourage her to 9 months later, bless us with the next generation, our precious grandson David.

So, what do I believe is this tug that serves me well at times and could also lead me astray? I believe it is the dominant way I am wired. It is neither good nor bad, it's just the way I respond to the world around me. It's a feeling in my heart. Simply put, it just feels like a tug. A pull that I believe through grace led me to the One who designed me with it. My Lord and Savior Jesus Christ. Obviously, my life in Christ has not been an arrival to a state of perfection or nirvana. In actuality my life with Him has been a continuation of a transforming process He started before I was born. Although sometimes painful and challenging, I somehow know in this process I am held secure in His unconditional love, strength and presence.

A process that still continues to lead me to rescue, only today it is the rescuing of convalescing older dogs and dogs with special needs, accompanied by a desire to help survivors of Human Trafficking. Most importantly, all taking place at the same time, is my family whom I adore and has continued to grow. My two oldest daughters have given me my two sons-in-law, and a total of three grandchildren. As for "The Tug" it's constant- it's part of my core identity and along with its Creator, takes me on daily little adventures. I love being wired for rescue, but mostly I have learned to trust and love the One who wired me.

So, how do you believe you're wired? Perhaps it's time to ask the One who wired you and see what happens next...could very well be another tiny tug.

About Mary Jane Piedra

 A passionate follower of Christ, Mary Jane Piedra loves to serve in any capacity where she sees a need. Currently her primary advocacy efforts lie in the abolishment of Human Trafficking by serving as an Advisory Board member of The Elite Foundation. She also for the past eight years along with her husband has been dedicated to the adoption, fostering and networking of convalescing and special needs dogs. She is highly regarded and respected in the South Florida community by many Animal Rescue organizations and local shelters.

As Founder of The Bahama Babies Relief Fund she received a personal commendation from First Lady Christie for coming to the aid of babies in crisis during the aftermaths of Hurricane Jeanne and Frances, which devastated Grand Bahama Island in 2004.

She was born and raised in Miami, Florida to Cuban parents where she also studied and holds a Bachelor of Science degree in Hospitality Management from Florida International University. In pursuit of her passion to help survivors of trauma she recently earned Certification in GCT Life Coaching, which she continuously practices in her daily life, not only with others but in her own personal growth.

She loves living life one day at a time with the ever-present knowledge of her saviors love for others and herself. She shares that love first and foremost with her wonderful Husband, three amazing daughters, sons in law and three grandchildren who all remain close living in South Florida.

You can connect with her on her Facebook page Mary Jane Piedra and through Instagram #maryj_piedra.

Creating Your 'New Normal'

Taking Life's Great Setbacks & Repurposing Them into Your Greatest Setups

By: Cristina Conte Lopez

I'd like to confess one thing about myself from the start: I am an optimist. I've been given a gift from God to see the potential good in bad situations. When life gives me lemons, through faith in action, I try to turn them into lemonade. That's a good thing for me because my life hasn't been easy. Maybe you can relate?

For about 10 years, I attended a large church in Ft. Lauderdale, Florida. The pastor was a skinny, charismatic guy with a squeaky voice. He was a great storyteller and a gifted communicator. But most of all, he was funny. And I noticed over time that he used humor to his advantage. Pastor Bob would get away with saying some of the most "in your face," spiritually challenging things because he knew how to weave humor and truth to bring about conviction. That also is a good thing because life can get pretty intense at times, and humor can soften the blows.

It was August 21st, 1992. Just a couple of days before Hurricane Andrew, the most destructive Category 5 hurricane in Florida's history, was predicted to hit the island where my Dad and I lived. Word spread throughout my community that all homes and businesses must be boarded up. A mandatory evacuation was in order. I rushed home to help my Dad hang up our huge, 10 feet tall, hurricane shutters. Only to find my father standing at the tippy top of an over-sized ladder, trying to attach a heavy aluminum panel to a concrete wall with nothing but a roll of Scotch tape! My suspicions were confirmed: My Dad had the beginnings of Alzheimer's disease.

Can you imagine the thoughts that flooded my mind when I saw my Dad on that ladder? He was fear-stricken. I could see it in his eyes. The impending hurricane had clouded his mind with confusion. But what about me? I too was flooded with fear – seeing that my Dad's ability to reason and find logic had been highjacked by a disease. I mean, honestly? Like Scotch tape is really going to hold up a 20 lbs. aluminum hurricane shutter?

I'd spend the next 16 years, as the disease ran its course, trying to process this "in your face," spiritually challenging illness. My friends were busy finishing up college and looking forward to an exciting future. I was busy trying to make sense of it all, in a way that felt authentic to my own pain, while simultaneously honoring to my Dad's life. A sense of humor and my faith in action were the tools that I used to protect myself from growing bitter towards God, and life in general, through this process.

If we live long enough, we will see that life is going to bring us great joys and deep sorrows. Life throws us a combination of curve balls and perfect pitches. Those curve balls have the potential to strike us out. But this story is about repurposing those setbacks, those bad breaks, into life's greatest setups. It's about seeing the

Bigger Picture and drawing our strength from a long-term perspective or a bird's eye view. This reminds me of the promise God gives us in Romans 8:28. It says, "And we know that God works all things together for the good of those who love Him."

This verse assures us that no matter the amount of good and evil that life throws our way, He is able to tip the scales, over and over, in our favor. No, not all things that happen to us, individually, are going to be good. It's impossible to think that each life event, situation or circumstance will always register in our minds as having been a positive one. But God *is promising* that He has the power to miraculously weave the sum of our experiences, both the positive and negative ones, for our ultimate good. Why? Because we love Him.

Last week, I was at the University of Miami's Lowe Art Museum with my daughter Belen's homeschool class. On the wall, there was a large, hand-woven tapestry on display. I was drawn to it because of its beauty. On the front side, what my eye could see was an intricately woven, elaborate design, rich in color and perfect in detail. But out of curiosity, I gently touched the corner and flipped it over to see its back side. I was surprised to see something very different. In stark contrast, the back of the tapestry was full of loose strings, bulky knots, and random patches.

I made the connection between God's promise in Romans 8:28, and how He is going to accomplish it. God is the Master Weaver. We are His vibrant threads. We don't see what He is doing behind the scenes with our pain, shame and mistakes. But in His hands, those things turn into a masterpiece. With that being said, would you allow me to encourage your heart with a few comeback stories that I'd like to share? Where should I start?

I'll begin by saying that bad things happen to good people. It's a fact. No one deserves for bad things to happen, but they do. Even if we make all the right choices, buy extra insurance, and live in a gated community, heartache is sure to find us at some point. When it does, allow yourself to feel the pain, let it surface, and try to address it. Don't ignore it or sweep it under the rug. This is part of living a real and authentic life. Living authentically begins with being ourselves, not an imitation of what we think we should be, feel, or do. So, when pain, with its many faces, enters our reality, be mindful of its presence and power. That is what I found myself doing as my father's Alzheimer's worsened. But after a proper time of healing, start taking baby steps toward moving on; toward **Creating Your "New Normal."**

Emotionally healthy people flow through these steps naturally. But beware! Some curve balls or set backs are harder to recover from than others. If you aren't careful, you may get too comfortable in the pit you're in. You may even find a new identity there. I know I almost did!

It was am on April 30th, 2011. My sister Mimi was knocking at my front door frantically. "Hurry up! Bring the Do Not Resuscitate documents!" she told me. My husband Tony had slept at the hospital. He was to undergo surgery in the morning but had taken an unexpected turn for the worse. Tony died an hour later. He had lost his 3-year fight against lung cancer. He was only 47.

The following two years proved to be a long, drawn-out season of grief for me. After his death, I had lost my identity. Thankfully, I continued to be an optimist. I could see some flashes of good that, one day, might spring forth from my grief-ridden situation. But my new identity became "the widow with the 3 little kids." Erroneously, I felt like I wore a label, written in **thick black Sharpie marker**, across my forehead that read: **WIDOW & 3 KIDS.** I felt alone and vulnerable. But then I did something impulsive!

One morning, I took my Mom Car, a mint green Volvo XC SUV, to CarMax for its routine service. As I waited for the work to get done, I perused the car lot. Three hours later, the kids and I drove home in a racy, "kind of new", navy blue BMW. It was fast and fun! And I'm not going to lie; it helped to lift my spirits. The funny thing with me buying the new Beamer was that not only did I ditch my SUV Mom Car, I also ditched the widow label too. Well, not entirely. Trust me, that "label" or new-found identity had its perks. One time, driving up to Georgia, I got out of a very pricey speeding ticket because of my "widow" status. My kids will shamelessly tell you, "Mom pulled out the 'widow card' and the state trooper let us off the hook!" All joking aside, life can get pretty intense at times. Try introducing some light-hearted humor, especially if you have small children. It softens its blows.

Almost 8 years have passed since Tony's death. These are some of the funnier stories that I choose to retell. But the truth is, for the first two years, I was stuck in my grieving process. Instead of inching my way out of the pit, I chose to remain stagnant. Instead of Creating a New Normal for the kids and I, I stayed comfortable in my pain. Everything in me was being tempted to sit back, pitch a tent in my Wounded Wilderness, and nurse my battle scars just a little bit longer. That is, until someone was brave enough to speak words of truth into my life.

Maybe you can relate to wanting to hold on to a label, like divorced or abused, for longer than necessary? Moving on doesn't mean the pain didn't happen; it just means *it no longer defines you.* Remember, the goal is to overcome life's setbacks so we can use them as the catalyst or spring board for our greatest setups.

Matthew Kelly, a New York Times Bestselling Author, says it like this in his book The Biggest Lie in the History of Christianity:

"Every time you become a better version of yourself, the consequences of your transformation echo throughout your family, friends, business, school, neighborhood, church, marriage, nation, and beyond – to people and places in the future."

"It is God who does the transforming, but only to the extent that **we cooperate.** So, our cooperation with God's desire to transform us is essential; it is the variable."

That's a sobering thought. Matthew Kelly says that we are "the variable." God is willing to co-labor with us in doing the transformative work, but we cast the deciding ballot. It's up to us if we stay stuck in our pit or not. But if you are reading this book, which is called <u>Unstoppable</u> that means you're on a mission. There is no cookie cutter answer as to how to cooperate with God Almighty in your transformation process, but may I offer some suggestions that have worked for me?

Find a quiet place where you feel safe to ask your inner self some deep questions. Like, what's holding me back? Or, what am I afraid of? The silent words you hear responding back to you should come from a place of love, not judgement. But by the same token, the words from the Spirit aren't always laced with sugar and spice, and everything nice. There may be some sort of call to action. Or something that sounds uncomfortable. Let's face it; to be transformed implies you're willing to engage in a potentially painful process in order to go to a higher level. That's probably why we resist taking those first steps toward it. It's like a toddler who refuses to use the potty; change can be messy, and it sometimes stinks!

Here's how this process played-out for me:

It was now 2013. Two years after Tony's death, and I found myself stuck and stagnated in the grieving process. One day,

42

something must have triggered it, but I became keenly aware within my soul that I was disturbed. So, I decided to quiet myself in prayer. I asked myself, "What's bothering you, Cristina?" At first, I heard my spirit telling me that I felt: offended, embarrassed, ashamed, and misunderstood. Then my mind went to a recent conversation with my nephew, Reggie. I was crying to him over something related to feeling overwhelmed now that I was a single mom. I wasn't expecting his response. Instead of allowing me to continue drowning behind the labels that I had given myself, (i.e. Widow and Single Mom), he did something different. Reggie compassionately, yet assertively reminded me that two full years had passed since Tony's death. It was time to leave those labels behind and start **Creating a New Normal** for the kids and me. Ouch! That was an unexpected curve ball.

So, going back to the original question: How did I cooperate with God in my transformation process? First, I went to a quiet place to pray and listen to the Spirit within. Feelings of embarrassment and shame surfaced, and it led me to remembering the conversation with my nephew. Did I hear Reggie's words coming from a place of love? At first, I didn't; quite the opposite. I felt embarrassed and judged. What did this 26-year-old kid know about being a widow or a single mom? I stayed in an attitude of prayer and invited the Spirit to speak to my pain.

A subtle shift in perspective happened. I was able to push my ego aside and discern Truth. I realized for myself that Reggie wasn't being judgmental; he was speaking from a place of love. What did he have to gain from hurting me? If there was anyone in my circle of influence that had earned the right to speak into my life, it was him. He had a track record of being caring, supportive and loyal. Why would his character suddenly change? This is how *I knew* it was constructive feedback, and not a criticism.

Remember, the goal is to take life's setbacks and repurpose them as we use them as the catalyst or spring board for our greatest setups. What about you? Here are some reminders that may prove helpful when you're ready to answer that question for your own life.

Tools To Creating Your New Normal

Be open:

- To using humor to soften life's blows.
- To putting faith into action.
- To accepting that bad things happen to good people.
- To living an authentic life.
- To feeling your pain; letting it surface; and addressing it.
- To moving forward with baby steps toward a New Normal.
- To identifying the limiting "labels" we can hide behind.
- To listening to what may sound like criticism but is intended as constructive feedback.

- To cooperating with God in your transformation process.

- To leaving behind the old thoughts, words and actions that are no longer serving us.

- And most importantly, to trusting whole-heartedly what God promises us in Romans 8:28. **"And we know that God works *ALL THINGS* together for the good of those who love Him."**

You are Unstoppable!

About Cristina Conte Lopez

Cristina Conte Lopez is an author, Spanish radio host, entertaining storyteller, an Optavia wellness coach and licensed psychotherapist with a private practice for women in Coral Gables, Florida. Cristina has multiple advanced degrees in communications, Spanish and clinical Social Work. She has a lifelong passion for personal growth and spiritual healing. Cristina uniquely weaves her Hispanic flare through storytelling & teaching, while incorporating the principles of transformational psychology. Her goal is to educate & inspire women of all ages to maximize their potential and pursue the lives they desire.

Although trained in areas such as Family Systems Therapy and Cognitive Behavior Modification, her greatest education has come from being a wife and mother of 5 children. At the age of 42, Cristina widowed and was left to raise her 3 young children. She later moved to Miami, Florida where she married her new love, together they have 5 children in their blended home. She is training to be a Classical Conversations Foundation's Tutor. Cristina has been a Foster Parent & Adoptive Parent with **4KIDS of South Florida**

Cristina sees herself as a Psycho-Educational Coach and is a big advocate of creating balance within the Six Main Areas of a

Woman's Life: Family, Faith, Finances, Food & Fitness, Fun & Friends, Future & Focus.

Cristina has been featured on multiple radio shows and she has hosted her own Spanish radio show for women called *Shine On Sister/Brilla Mi Hermana* on Almavision 87.7 FM.

To work with Cristina, she can be reached at CCLopez.com

Sprinkle It Everywhere

By: Julietta Wenzel

I want you to feel loved. I want you to know that you matter. I want you to love yourself. I want you to know that you are perfect. I want you to know that when you give this gift to yourself, you give it to the world, as well. I want you to know that this will change the world. I want you to help me change the world.

As a little girl growing up in Wisconsin when I was asked the question, "What do you want to be when you grow up?", I always confidently answered that, I wanted to be a hairdresser. I wanted to be just like the two women I admired most in the world, my mom and Ganny. These women showed me the importance of caring for others. They taught me that community mattered and that we should help others where we could. They taught me to be generous with sharing kindness and compassion. These women always found a way to make others feel loved and appreciated. They touched the hearts of many. They showed how a tiny gesture could have a giant impact. I feel very honored to have been raised by them.

One day, when I was a little bit older my mom shocked me by telling me there was no way she was going to allow me to be a hairdresser, because I was way too smart for that. I knew I wanted to help people, and as a young girl the most helping profession I could think of was of a doctor. That was now my answer to the question kids get asked all the time, what are you going to be when you grow up? I was going to be a doctor.

I enjoyed thinking about becoming a doctor. I loved science and math classes and I got good grades, so I didn't think it would be difficult. As I got older, I started realizing exactly what I would have to do to become a doctor. School was always very easy for me, but I didn't particularly like it. Thinking about all the years I would have to go to school made becoming a doctor less and less appealing.

Growing up we ate dinner together as a family at the kitchen table every night. At dinner we would talk. No television. No cell phones. Just the four of us sharing time and conversation together. As a child I thought that every family spent time together talking and having dinner together. Flash forward a few years and I discover how lucky I was to be blessed with a family that was loving, supportive and connected.

One night at dinner my dad asked me if I had ever thought of becoming a Physical Therapist instead of a doctor. I had never heard of a Physical Therapist. I had no idea what a Physical Therapist did. My dad gave me a brief description, and it sounded like a great alternative to becoming a doctor.

This took place in the days before the internet and Google, so I had to do a little work to find out more about this physical therapy stuff. I made a trip to the local library and started doing my research. Everything that I read about physical therapy made it sound like the perfect career for me. Best of all, it was a bachelor's program, so I would only have to do 4 years of college. I was set, I was going to become a Physical Therapist!

What I failed to learn through my research was that because of the number of people applying for the same program, it was harder to get into Physical Therapy (PT) school than medical school. The school I planned to attend, University of Wisconsin-Madison, only accepted 60 of the thousands that applied to the Physical Therapy program each year. This resulted in lots of stress, sleepless nights, and searches for my next career choice, in case I didn't get accepted into PT school. Fortunately, my grades were good enough and I made the cut. I finished school and passed my boards with flying colors ready to jump into the healthcare system helping people heal.

I started my career in healthcare believing that it was first and foremost about the patients and doing what was best for them. I thought that it was filled with people who had chosen to be in healthcare because they cared about people and wanted to help them. The more time passed, the more I was to discover how wrong my assumptions had been.

In the realm of treating pain, the treatments that patients are guided to most often are toxic medicines, painful injections and dangerous surgeries. It amazes me that people do not understand that most medications do not heal the body, they just control the symptoms. They also have side effects, some of which can be very dangerous. The cortisone injections over time eat away at the soft tissues. Some surgeries are necessary, but there is growing evidence that shows that a large percentage of orthopedic surgeries are not needed. In fact, better outcomes can be achieved with less invasive treatments such as Physical Therapy. Surgeries also create scar tissue which can have long term implications throughout the body, not just at the surgical site. Once you have been cut, you can't be uncut.

The results of the treatments mentioned are often short term at best. They do not address the true cause of the problem but are only symptom management. Because of this, the problem often returns or shows up someplace else in the body. There are many natural healing options that can get to the root cause of the problem and support the body in healing itself. Fortunately, over the years and thanks to greater access to information, more people are becoming aware of other options to heal their bodies.

There are indeed many people in healthcare who are compassionate, caring beings, who are there to support people's health and healing needs. However, I also have found that many are there only for the paycheck. Administration cares first about finances, not what's best for the patient. When I started my career, patients could get all the care they needed to recover from injury or surgery, but as time passed treatment allotments decreased. As the years passed not only did the number of treatments given decrease, but the therapists were being required to treat more patients in less time, often treating multiple patients simultaneously.

Further, as therapists we were also encouraged to only use evidence-based medicine. If the treatment wasn't supported by research, it shouldn't be used. It's not uncommon to be criticized or laughed at by others in the healthcare field for using treatments that have not been proven by research. What is frequently ignored is that often research is manipulated by those that are paying for the research. Therefore, the results may not be accurate, but rather just supporting the money trail.

The fact that there has been no formal research done to support something does not mean that it does not work. Things must exist before they can be researched. If we only use treatments that have been proven effective by research, we will always be stuck in the past. If I see results happening in my clinic, then is that not evidence that it works? If we never try something that has not been proven by research, we will never forge new territory. We have not found all the answers yet, and the only way to do so is to try new things.

The other aspect of caring for patients that did not feel right to me was that I was encouraged to not get too connected with my patients. I was told that if you did, patients would then become dependent on you. That it was not healthy to get close to your patients and would only result in problems.

None of this felt right to me. Patients are human beings, not widgets in a factory. Each one is unique, and their problems are unique to them. Every person has a history of what brought them to have the problem they deal with. They are body, mind and spirit, and you can't avoid addressing all three and expect true healing to happen. Healthcare was missing the greatest healing power there is, and that is love.

When I was a new graduate working at a hospital with many very experienced PTs, I couldn't understand why patients preferred to work with me. I also couldn't understand why patients would walk much further and with less help when they walked with me. If techniques and experience were what mattered most, then the patients should be doing better with the other therapists. What was the difference between the treatment they received from me versus the other therapists? My conclusion.... love.

Everything is energy. Each energy has its own frequency. The energy of love is the most healing frequency. If you want to improve the outcome of your treatment, you just need to add love. I suspect that almost every problem that exists in the world today is due to a shortage of love.

Speaking with people about love has been interesting. Some tell me that love is something that they will only share with their family and closest friends. Some have a hard time considering love outside the romantic realm. Many believe it is something that you must share sparingly.

I would ask you to consider that love is something that should be shared abundantly. Anywhere there is a problem, adding love will improve the situation. It's not something to hold on to. Love is meant to be given freely to others and to ourselves. Love is limitless.

It does not need to be conserved. The more you share love, the more it multiplies.

I was not happy working in the traditional PT world. When the opportunity presented itself, I got to create my own clinic with another PT. This has provided me the space to practice in the way that feels right to me. I have been able to integrate alternative techniques into my practice that support healing the whole patient, body, mind and spirit. Some call it, "working outside the box." I say there is no box.

Practicing this way brings clients to me who report they have tried everything else, but nothing has helped. In my clinic we get to explore different areas that can be contributing to the patient's problem. The pain and dysfunction are just the symptoms. They are not the actual problem. We get to be open to what shows up in the session to address. It might be muscle, bones, or joints that we address or connective tissue and scars. It's also possible that the energetic highways of the body (acupuncture meridians) need balancing. Sometimes what comes up is emotions. They can be from the present or the past. The past sometimes even means a past life.

Every day in the clinic I find weak muscles become strong by addressing emotions. I find tight muscles instantly become flexible when the emotion connection to it is addressed. It is obvious to me and the client that a physical problem has been corrected with a non-physical solution. I am not sure how research will ever be able to measure and analyze this work, but my clients are pleased with the results.

I also believe we are one. I am because you are. I acknowledge each person who lies on my treatment table for the work they are doing. Each piece they heal in themselves helps heal everyone. One of the most common problems I see is that people struggle to love themselves. Each person that can begin to love themselves helps us all get closer to loving ourselves. If we can all love ourselves unconditionally, I believe hate, anger and violence will vanish. These things cannot exist where love lives. Parents who are not loving themselves are teaching their children not to love themselves. When a parent loves themselves, they become better parents and model self-love for their children. Imagine a world where all children grew up knowing self-love?

Sometimes ancestral patterns are revealed during sessions. When we can heal that ancestral pattern, it is possible to heal it through all space and time so that the pattern is broken and no longer gets to be repeated through our lineage. Imagine how good it feels to clear negative patterns for your entire family.

How do we research love? How do we measure love? What if all the treatments we provided did nothing, but it was the love that they were administered with that produced the outcome? I don't know that these questions can be answered, but I do know that by bringing love to my work, I have enjoyed doing what I do for almost 30 years, and my clients appear to feel the same.

How does love show up in the clinic? First, by truly caring about the patient. See the human first, not their diagnosis. The outcomes should matter for the client's wellbeing, not to feed the ego of the practitioner who thinks they fixed them. I cannot fix my clients; I can only support and guide them to heal themselves. Healing is an inside job.

Choose modalities that support healing, not just symptom management. The techniques I use most in my clinic are the Voila Method, Microcurrent Point Stimulation and Craniosacral Therapy, because they address not just the physical body, but the emotional and energetic aspects of the client as well.

Hugs are given freely. Some argue that hugs are too personal or may be taken the wrong way. I find them to be healing and supportive. They also give the client an opportunity to express their gratitude for your support in their healing.

The environment of the clinic can also emanate love. Warm inviting colors, beautiful art, healing essential oil scents, and warm and friendly support staff all make a huge difference in how the space feels. When patients tell you how comfortable your office is and how much they enjoy speaking with your staff you know you are on the right track.

I hope to inspire others in the healthcare industry to bring love to the game. Let's show up for our clients like we would show up for our loved ones. This is how we heal the world. Yes, science and research has given us amazing discoveries that have helped countless people, but that doesn't mean we need to exclude love. Love and science are not mutually exclusive. I believe that when we add love to science our outcomes will be greater than was ever thought possible.

Let's not stop with adding love to healthcare. Let's sprinkle it everywhere. Sprinkle it generously. How can you add love to your profession and to all other aspects of your life? What can be achieved when you do? Let's create magic together by changing the world with love.

About Julietta Wenzel

 Julietta Wenzel, PT is committed to creating a world is that it is Loving, Kind, Compassionate, Connected and Empowered. You will almost always find a smile on her face because she is grateful for everything. She grew up in Wisconsin when kids played outside until the streetlights came on. She graduated with a degree in Physical Therapy from the University of Wisconsin-Madison. After graduating she worked in many different settings before deciding to open her own clinic. She presently co-owns two private practice clinics in the Fort Lauderdale area where she works with children and adults from all over the globe.

Her dedication to find the best techniques to support people in their healing journey has led her to study Voila Method, Myofascial Release, Craniosacral Therapy, and Visceral Manipulation, Micro-Current Point Stimulation (MPS), Therasuit, MEDEK, Redcord, and Quantum Reflex Integration. To inspire other therapists to bring holistic treatment options to their practice she teaches Voila Method and Microcurrent Point Stimulation both in the US and internationally.

When she is not busy treating patients or teaching, she is making healing crystal art and jewelry known as SoulCandy or planning underground dining experiences for her group called Foodie Freaks. Her experience as an exchange student also gave her a love of travel. Connecting with and learning from other cultures has had a big influence on her life. Her experience is that the language of love, kindness and compassion is understood and appreciated everywhere.

Connect with Julietta at http://oceantherapycenter.com

GOING THROUGH LIFE AS A TEENAGER

By: Miranda Parma-Vera

In sharing my experiences as a teenager, I want to help others understand what it might be like for someone younger living in this generation. Someone who has to deal with being pressured, someone who has to deal with emotional pain, and someone who has to live during a time when the value of life doesn't mean much. This is my journey over the past 2 years.

When you're little you don't think about how hard life is going to be or how hard life is, it is the time for laughter, fun, and always being happy. As you grow up you look at being a teenager as such an exciting thing and it can be...sometimes.

When I became a teenager, I had no idea how it would affect my mind, heart, and body. By the time I had become an "official" teenager, I was attending a Christian school. This school was chosen by my parents, because it was also the location of where we attended church. I had no idea how hard life would become for me even in such a professed safe environment.

I had been bullied since I was younger. The first bully interaction was in the second grade and it's funny because I can just look back at it now and laugh, but what was coming my way was no laughing matter. It was the beginning of ninth grade my first year in high school and I was over the moon excited. I had all my goals laid out and I was ready to be an excelling student and make many great friends. Everything was going tremendously well until the middle of my ninth-grade year. It was at this time, that a girl started to be tough on me and I didn't think much of it at first because we had been acquaintances and I had always been friendly towards her.

However, one day things got out of control, at lunch the girl decided to hit me in the face with a water bottle, over and over and over again. She didn't stop. It was the longest lunch period of my life! I was moving around, to avoid her, and she would follow me and hit me in the head with the water bottle repeatedly, I was so beyond annoyed. Then waiting to be allowed back into the classrooms the girl got in my face, telling me I was a pathetic liar and she kept getting closer, continuing to hit me in the head with a water bottle. She and the friend that was with her were about an inch from my face and I couldn't take it anymore. With careless judgment I pushed her away from me. I didn't want to fight her, but I didn't want to let her keep tormenting me either. There were no teachers around the only people around were students and my friends that were just standing there laughing. The girl threw her backpack down and started cursing me out getting ready to fight, so I walked away. I did not want to be part of the drama she was about to create. She and her friend followed me as I walked away and got in my face once again, no one was there for me, I felt so alone.

My friends would tell me later that she was just kidding. For the next couple weeks, she and her friends spread rumors about me making every single person in my grade hate me including people I had been very close with. My parents were there for me as much as they could be, because I really did not want them involved. The situation was very difficult for me, because I was afraid of the possible outcomes.

Finally, my parents convinced me to go to a teacher or someone in authority at the school to tell them of what was going on. I hadn't told anyone about the situation at school, because I was not open about my emotions especially about those that hurt the most. My family and I went to the administration of the school; and they sent us away.

Then I talked to a teacher and she was the only support system I had other than my family of course. She was great to talk to but sadly no matter what I said she could not do anything about the situation. The girl and her friends continued to torment me and ruined many of my relationships in school.

I didn't think things could get any worse until I broke my foot and people did not believe me for one second. At first, I had to makeshift something to support my foot because the one boot I had was broken on the bottom. Of course, people started every rumor they could about this. Then I finally couldn't bear a sock with medical tape wrapped around it anymore, so I tapped up my boot and wore it, but the rumors continued.

Finally, I was able to get my cast and people made up the dumbest rumors and everyone believed them. The most annoying rumor that everyone believed was that I had made my cast out of paper mâché. The situation in school remained hard until the end of the year after which I finally got to leave the school; I had been attending for 5 years. All of this bullying and drama had emotionally damaged me for so long. My family let me decide to homeschool for the following school year. I can say it has been the best decision I have ever made. Although at the time it seemed like I was running away from the problem, I had to decide to look at the situation, as it is now, an opportunity to grab a hold of my life and succeed on my own.

From this bully interaction I learned, sometimes it's okay to hurt and feel, it will shape you and teach you a new way to become independence. I'm truly thankful that I went through this and God guided me through the rest of that year. This verse truly helped me through this past year, "before I was afflicted, I went astray, but now I keep your word. You are good and do good; teach me your statutes."-Psalms 119:67-68

Another thing you never think will happen as a teenager, is all the worldly problems that you think you would face when you are an adult. My first taste of the real world was again in a Christian environment, I was at a youth camp and was with many close friends. I had always known people don't always have it easy, but I never knew how what I was about to be told was going to affect me.

We were in the middle of a worship song and one of my friends was missing but my friends and I did not think much of it because there were over a thousand kids in the auditorium. My close friend at the time and I received a call from our friend, he told us that he was at the football field and was going to try and kill himself by jumping off the top of the bleachers. My heart shattered.

My friend and I immediately grabbed an adult and ran to find our friend. We made it in time before anything happened, but this experience changed my point of view on life forever. I don't even recall telling anyone about this. It took a tremendous toll on me, because it made me realize that life could end at one moment and also that people have the power to take their own lives in matters of seconds and that sometimes there's nothing you can do to help.

Although I did not tell anyone about what had happened right away, sometimes it feels better to keep to yourself for a while. It may not seem like the healthiest choice, but it allows you to fully feel what just happened and sometimes you need to feel even the most painful things to understand and gain new knowledge from life lessons.

Sometimes you're not fully prepared for things even when you may think you are. I wasn't prepared to lose a friend to suicide; and I was not prepared for a situation that was actually quite ironic seeing as though my mom is one of the Founders of a foundation that works with survivors of sex trafficking. My family and I had gone on a cruise for Christmas and my sister and I made friends on the ship. Our parents knew where we were every second of everyday. They knew that we were hanging out with a group of friends around the ship, but the group of people got larger, as the days passed. On the second to last night of the cruise, there was an older couple that had been hanging around with us, they were older, but enjoyed dancing with us and were having a great time. I also had fun spending my time with a friend, who was older, but she was young at heart.

The man that was part of the couple, one day came up to me and my friend; and wrapped us with a cloth and kept pulling us closer and closer to him. We both danced away, as soon as we perceived it getting sexual. Eventually, we all got tired and sat down and we didn't think anything of it. But then we noticed that the guy had a little too much to drink. He started flirting with me and many of the other girls at the table but then he singled me out and started to hit on me.

I became very uncomfortable and walked away and went to my room. Later that night, I found out that he tried to fight my sister because she was defending me and standing up for herself. My sister stood up to the guy, telling him that his behavior wasn't right and that I was her kid sister.

The last night on the cruise there was another dance party and the couple had not been seen together for a while. Without the couple around, my sister and I were dancing with our friends like customary. My sister had told my dad what had happened the night prior. She and my parents didn't know but I was still overwhelmed with fear and a very nasty emotion, I didn't want to talk about the situation. Before the night was over, the guy from the couple showed up at the party, but this time my dad took charge and defended my sister and me. I saw what a true family man looked like that day. My dad was looking out for the family and making sure that this guy would never ever come near us again. My outlook on family truly changed from that moment. A family can be made up of different people, but family looks out for each other and protects one another no matter what they have to do. This was a brush experience and I learned that even though I knew that there are men, who will try things with younger girls, you don't notice it when you are having fun. Thank God I had my sister and father to protect me, but the nasty feeling stayed with me for a while.

Then at the beginning of the new year, on Valentine's day, February 14, 2018 there was a shooting at Stoneman Douglas High School this truly hit home for me. Dealing with my friend that had tried to kill himself was bad enough but now to have this happen truly broke me down inside. Knowing that someone took the lives of people I knew, and the fact that he was close to my age was incredibly unthinkable in my mind.

I had always known that there were people out there who enjoyed hurting others, but I didn't think it would happen so close to home. I had experienced a lockdown before at my old school, because there was a reported gunman on campus, but fortunately, it was just a false alarm. When the Stoneman Douglas shooting happened at first, all I could think of is, "I hope everyone is okay."

But, then a whole bunch of social media pictures and videos were posted of kids bleeding, crying and screaming. Then a few hours later, it was all over the news, and I recognized a few of the kids and one of them I had been friends with. The false alarm I had been through, actually was real for those kids and they lost their lives.

I cannot believe how insensitive and inhumane people can be during these tragic times, no matter what happens in the world even if it's bad there will always be someone who wants to publicize images of pain when it should be private. I attended the memorial for my friend, and a reporter took pictures of me, even though my parents told them not to do it. They were more concerned with getting their picture than how it was affecting me and others at the service. Those pictures of me circulated all over social media.

The mass shooting left a hole in my life and since I have been very fearful, I still am. Growing up in a generation where killing and hurting others doesn't mean anything is sick. People are growing up knowing how to kill. We see it whether through video games, violent movies, social media or on the news. I still don't have any idea how to take control of this fear and maybe I shouldn't.

My teenage life so far has been a roller coaster and I am only 16. I can tell you personally that it is easier looking at someone else's life and being able to see if there's an issue, but it is not an easy thing to do it for yourself.

The same year of all this tragedy, I experienced my first relationship. I had an interest in a guy, apparently, this guy had been 'in like with me' since the beginning of the year. We began hanging out and getting to know each other. I brought him to meet my family and I met his mother. Our parents let us hang out we were together for about 5 months before he broke up with me. He had given me a whole bunch of reasons to why he could not be with me anymore and it broke my heart. The next day though I saw him flirting and being touchy with other girls and my heart broke further. I had always been good at telling my sister whether her boyfriends were going to hurt her before they did and every time, I was 100% right. But, when it happened to me, I couldn't differentiate for myself, I was not prepared for a relationship.

The pressure to do things and the pressure to feel things that you don't truly feel was not something I was prepared for. Luckily, I stood strong and knew that I wanted my life to be special. I didn't want to give up things that are supposed to be special at such a young age. Especially, because even now I do not feel prepared to share my life because I don't feel I have it under control. My first actual relationship taught me to stand strong for what I believe in for myself.

Being a teenager, I've learned a number of different things. One that even though your parents try to prepare you for life, there are certain things that cannot be taught and have to be learned through experiences. I don't think that my parents could have imagined that they would have to prepare me for bullying, to deal with suicide and senseless murders. I know that since I was little, my parents have done all they could to prepare me to be a successful young woman that will make mistakes, but who will learn from them and succeed.

I know many of you reading are either parents, siblings, or maybe even someone who looks after young children. I don't necessarily wish these things would have never happened, because I am grateful for the life lessons I learned. However, as a teenager sometimes we are very head strong and more than likely this prevents us from opening up and letting others in to help us. I never knew how hard it would be to talk about the things going on in my life especially with those close to me. You may feel as though you can't do anything but just being nice and caring about someone and being able to give your shoulder and to listen means the world.

We teens, are not always going to open up, that doesn't necessarily mean we don't want to talk to you, but it could mean we either don't have everything laid out or fully understand that situation or we just don't know how to put things into words. Something that really helped me was having my special person. Someone who doesn't need for you to tell them what's wrong but just is there for you to cheer you up. This person was my sister, she and I have always had a special bond we don't normally have to talk to each other to know one of us is down and she was sort of my anchor without even knowing it.

In these past 2 years life has been a roller coaster, I have learned many hard life lessons. But my biggest lesson has been that life goes at its own pace and that you can either go on the ride or stay behind and wait for the next coaster, or you can decide to never let obstacles bring you down because in the long run they will help you. With that I leave you with this, "You never know how strong you are, until being strong is the only choice you have because you are unstoppable."

About Miranda Parma-Vera

Miranda Parma-Vera is a 16-year-old student who is homeschooled and going into her junior year of high school. She lives with her family in Florida and plans to graduate a year early. She is hoping that her chapter impacts and informs people about what may go on in a teenager's life. Miranda hopes to be involved in many other books after this and might even write her own. She is also very in touch with the right hemisphere of her brain and aspires to be creative with everything she does in life. She hopes to be able to build a platform for herself in the near future and believes that this chapter is the first step in doing so. She also hopes that her words can be used as a tool to share awareness in matters such a preventing suicide. Look out for the name Miranda Parma-Vera in the near future...

PART II

The Power of Surrender:

Cultivate Acceptance

The Process to the Promise

By: Nadine A. Raphael

I remember some years ago reading a story that has proven true in my own life. The story is about a man and a moth. A man found a cocoon of an emperor moth and took it home to watch it emerge. One day a small opening appeared, and for several hours the moth struggled but couldn't seem to force its body past a certain point. Deciding something was wrong, the man took scissors and snipped the remaining bit of the cocoon. The moth emerged easily. However, its body was large and swollen and its wings small and shriveled. The man waited with expectation that in a few hours the wings would spread open into its natural beauty. But instead of developing into a creature free to fly, the moth spent its life dragging around a swollen body on shriveled, underdeveloped wings. The constricting cocoon and the struggle necessary to pass through the tiny opening was God's creative way of forcing fluid from the body of the moth into its wings for development. The fact that it had wings was nature's promise that one day it would do what it was created to do, fly. But that promise came to a painful halt by a "merciful" snip. What looked like a painful process was exactly what the moth needed to develop its wings. (Author, Beth Landers)

If we were to be honest with ourselves, I think most of us would admit that we love short cuts. If I can take a short route instead of a long route and it brings me to the same destination in less time, sign me up immediately! But we know that the shortest route doesn't always equate to the best route. I've taken what I thought was a short cut only to meet upon a detour, a dead end or worst yet, traffic! Quicker isn't always better. Which is what the man learned, by cutting the moth's process he robbed it of its purpose.

Since I was a little girl, people have always told me that I was a natural leader. I, on the other hand, couldn't see it. Maybe because it was hard to see leadership through the lens of abuse that I experienced through-out most of my upbringing.

At around 22 years old my life radically changed. I was sentenced to almost six years in prison and while serving that prison sentence, God radically intercepted my life and totally altered its course. I discovered that not only did my life have meaning but it had a greater purpose than the horrible things I had experienced through-out my upbringing. This truth shifted my perspective of myself and my outlook on life. The thought that I was born with purpose inside of me and that God wanted to use that purpose to impact the world around me, was life giving to someone who always thought her life lacked significance. This new understanding brought me to new life. I no longer saw my prison environment through the lens of defeat, but I began to see all the opportunities around me to make a positive impact. I decided to make a difference right there, behind bars. I started a prison newsletter to encourage incarcerated mothers. I started teaching G.E.D. to inmates who never completed high school. I began a Bible study to help inmates find hope and strength through God's Word. Those prison years were some of the best years of my life experience because they were used to help me discover the leader within me. The leader I thought did not exist. I soon realized that prison was not what happened to me, but prison happened for me.

We all tend to listen to the lies that have been spoken over us. Worse yet are the ones we partner with and speak over ourselves. Lies like, you are nothing, you are stupid, you are a failure, you are an accident and the list can go on. Words can wound us deeply, damaging and distorting our perception of ourselves and others. These words of negativity will attempt to rob us of our purpose, paralyzing us with feelings of fear, inferiority and insignificance. To overcome words that keeps us stuck in pain or in a constant state of rejection, we must stop agreeing with these lies either verbally or mentally and replace them with God's truths. When we choose to partner with God's truth, we overrule the lies that have been planted in our minds. Truths like you are unique, you are one of a kind, you are valuable, you are loved, you are accepted, you are forgiven, you are chosen, you are purposed, and my favorite, you are free. Embracing these truths and living from that place, sets us up to walk out our God given destiny.

In prison I was constantly being told, by prison guards as well as outside visiting preachers and speakers, that my life would be used to have a profound influence upon many people not only in prison but those who are in the "free" world as well. I didn't know how but I gladly embraced those words.

After I was released from prison, I was so excited to go back to my hometown in New York City to make a difference. But times had changed during my years of incarceration and so did people. My transition from prison to home was a lonely road. It was not what I expected. Before long I began to desire the community and the security I once had with the ladies in prison.

After completing one year of continuous work, as required by the courts, I moved to Florida with my seven-year-old daughter. I immediately got hired for a position at a very large hotel chain. Months into the company I moved from the receptionist to be the assistant to the sales director of the South Florida region. Not too long after that I was promoted to Assistant Sales Manager. I was on an upward climb at a rapid pace. While I enjoyed my job and the growth within the company, I knew there was more to my life than what I was doing. But I became comfortable with what I was doing and started settling. Before long, my work became my security. My career achievements and the applause of those around me started to dim the pulse I once felt of a deeper call within me.

One day I received mail from a woman I had become good friends with while I was in prison. She was an older woman from Holland who was serving a life sentence and had already been incarcerated for 23 years. She lived her life with sheer grace and purpose while serving the rest of her life behind bars. The letter she wrote to me brought me to tears. The last sentence in her letter was, "Nadine you owe it to the world around you to not sit on what God has placed within you." I cried. I didn't know what to do with what she wrote. I couldn't understand how it was my responsibility to make something happen. What was I supposed to do? I mean after all I am the ex-prisoner with a felony, whose had all the cards stacked against me, my entire life. I was giving excuses because the right response to my friend's letter meant I had to do something with what I knew was in me and honestly, I was afraid. I think we talk ourselves out of God's promises for our lives because either they look too big or we just don't want the responsibility of having to do something with what's been entrusted to us.

After some time, I resigned from the hotel without having another job in queue. I was a single mother with a felony record and I just left my job at a well-known hotel chain while on an upward climb in the company. I know you're probably wondering, "what were you thinking Nadine?" I wondered the same thing. But I knew that I was making the right decision. I left that career scared but resolute in my decision. Barely two days later I received a call from my local church asking me if I would consider taking a position in their Business Office. They said they couldn't pay me much but was hoping I would consider. I never thought of myself working for a Church and yet for some reason I found myself at the interview on a Sunday morning saying yes to start working the following day. I can't explain it, but I had an overwhelming sense that every step I was taking, the move to Florida, resigning from the hotel and now taking the position at the church, were being divinely guided and orchestrated by God.

I started working in the Finance Department entering data, paying invoices and spending hours at a time standing over a copy machine making copies of hundreds of checks and receipts. My family thought that I was crazy and at times my human logic would kick in to agree with them. But for some reason I had a sense of peace in knowing that I was where I was supposed to be.

Little did I know God was using this season to develop my character. Yes, I was learning new skills but working in that office, making copies and filing receipts was teaching me how to remain faithful in the small. I didn't know at the time that what I was doing which seemed small and insignificant was actually monumental to my growth for what awaited me in the seasons ahead. As I've looked over my life, I've concluded that no season is ever a wasted season. Even seasons that seems like total barrenness are purposeful. Every season of life brings with it lessons to be learned, character to be developed, and new abilities to discover. This is all a part of the process. So often we fight the process because it's not what we planned. We want to give up, throw in the towel and walk away. But the part of our journey that seems most constricting and difficult maybe exactly what we need to develop the wings necessary to fly; to develop what we need to become who we are purposed to be.

After a while I started being asked to teach various classes. I started going into the local prisons to share my story with women and men who were serving time, some even on death row. I had entered several phases of God's promises for my life and I didn't realize it. My purpose was being lived out as I stepped out and said yes to the small opportunities leading to greater opportunities to serve the world around me.

Two years into me working as the assistant to the Business Administrator, my boss was transitioned out of his role and I was offered his position. This position would oversee the entire finances and Human Resources of the Church. I would be responsible for almost one hundred staff members, several residential properties, and the finances of both the school and church. I quickly turned down the position. Fear came to remind me that I was unqualified. But something within me kept tugging at me that the position was for me. But since I had already turned down the offer, I was certain they had already moved on to the next more qualified candidate. After three weeks the position was offered to me again and this time I said yes. I gave a bold yes with fear whispering in my ear to remind me that I was unworthy. Some people think fear is the worst thing. But fear isn't bad in and of itself. What is worse than fear is when we allow the fear to paralyze us and rob us of what God has for us. I said yes in spite of my fears. I served in the position as the Business Administrator at my Church for almost twelve years. That position helped to develop my leadership, stretch my dependence on God and enlarged my influence as a woman in leadership and pastor in a church of over 5000 people. I currently serve as the first Chief Operating Officer the church has ever had. I get the privilege of traveling around to countries to speak and help train and develop other pastors and leaders in ministry. I am humbled for the opportunity to speak and preach on a platform where my voice is used to impact so many lives just as it had been told to me many years ago.

None of this is because I am someone that had all the right cards dealt to her. As a matter of fact, quite the opposite is true. I was unwanted at birth. Abused physically, mentally and emotionally in my upbringing. I was a teenaged mom. Sentenced to almost six years in prison and have had to overcome layers of a poor self-image. However, I gave myself permission to embrace the process and not allow my past to become my identity.

Looking at my journey, I find that the process to the promise has phases that I would like to share with you that may help your perspectives when the journey gets filled with disappointments, delays and difficulties. Here are four common phases along the journey to our promise that I've experienced:

The Go Phase: In order to embrace something new you must be willing to let go of the old. In order to step into your next, you must be willing to step out from where you are. Going is hard because it requires you to leave your comfort zone. Going may not mean that you leave somewhere physically, but you may have to leave old mindsets, old attitudes, maybe old friendships or old lifestyle choices that you can't take with you into your next season of life. Some things we must choose to leave behind us in order to embrace not only what's ahead of us but also what's lying dormant within us.

The Lack Phase: At this phase in the process you realize that your security is gone. You left what you were accustomed to. What you used to depend on suddenly is no longer there. You are way beyond your comfort zone. At times you may feel lonely and ill equipped. But it is in this stage of lack where you begin to grow deep roots. Our deep roots are helping to build faith and belief within us. We must be careful in this stage not to allow the lack that we are experiencing to rob us of our belief that there is a promise up ahead. Your faith and belief will be important to the strength you need to keep going when you don't see the full promise being manifested.

The Abandon Phase: In this phase, just as you thought you were stepping into what you've been believing for and working toward, you run into unexpected challenges. The people you thought would be with you are suddenly turning away from you. The resources seem scarce and nonexistent. The road blocks and the challenges are making it too unbearable and you want to quit and run to the nearest exit. This phase typically happens just before the promise is manifested. I remember giving birth to my daughter. And just before she was about to come out, I told the doctor that I'm going to stop now and come back tomorrow to have the baby. The pain was so unbearable, I was losing my common sense! The wise doctor told me that I could leave after I pushed one more time. One last push and I was holding my daughter in my arms. Just before we reap a great reward, we are tempted to abandon the process. You must realize that what God has placed inside of you is bigger than you. If this promise was worth conceiving, then sure enough it is worth birthing. And if no one sees it the way you see it, it's ok because this promise wasn't placed inside of them, it was placed inside of you. So, don't abort what only you can deliver!

The Discovery Phase: After you've made it through the abandon phase you get to embrace the discovery of the promise. Your time to reap what you have sown and believed for is here and now you get to experience the fruit of your labor. While this fruitful phase is rewarding, you begin to realize that this process wasn't so much about the destination (the promise) as it was about the journey. It was never about arriving somewhere, but the entire process has been a journey of purpose for life. Purpose isn't merely a destination that is arrived at, but it's a journey of discovery that is constantly evolving allowing you to discover more of yourself and your responsibility to the world around you.

Regardless of where you are in your journey, just know that today is part of the process. The process may seem too long, and you're tempted to find a shortcut. But let me remind you that if you, shortcut the process you will shortchange yourself from becoming the person that the process is meant to develop and define along the way.

Happy trails on your process to your promise!

82

About Nadine Raphael

Nadine is an Author, Pastor and International Speaker. She is passionate about activating people to fulfill their God-given purpose, and potential.

Known for her bold, passionate, compelling style, Nadine loves taking her messages of hope and inspiration to people everywhere from Syrian Refugees in Europe fleeing from ISIS, to Leadership Trainings in the Caribbean, to Seminars, Church services, Graduation Commencements or Workshops. By sharing her story of overcoming hardships and finding purpose, she has impacted people from every walk of life to do the same. Whether women, men, accomplished, impoverished, hopeful or in despair, Nadine can relate to them and through her transparent and engaging communication, they can relate to her. Woven in every message is her belief that "everything you need to do what you have been purposed to do, is already in you."

In March 2018, Nadine released a memoir titled, "But God: Finding Purpose in Your Darkest Hour." This memoir chronicled her journey from prison to purpose. Written to encourage and inspire people to know that they can rise above their circumstances no matter how grim they may seem.

She is the Chief Operating Officer and Executive Pastor at Christian Life Center in Fort Lauderdale, Florida. A Church of 5000 people representing over 25 nationalities.

Nadine is happily married to her loving husband. Together they have three children, Tenae (26), Isaiah (14) Natacia (13) and two rambunctious dogs, Shakespeare and Katara.

Her favorite pass time are long scenic drives or just curling up on the couch with a good book in hand.

To contact Nadine Raphael :

Twitter, Facebook, Instagram is: @NadineAraphael

Website: nadinearaphael.com

Just Twenty-Four More Hours

By Kim Andy

March 7, 2012 – this is the day my life slammed into a brick wall. In that one moment in time, a split second, everything in my life, and what I thought I knew about life, changed.

I now belong to a club that I never thought I would be a part of. Things like this happen to other people, right? Something you may see on the news where you feel sad, but then you change the channel or keep scrolling and life goes on. This isn't something that could happen to me. This can't be real. Yet it was real, because there I was, picking out a coffin, a burial plot, planning a funeral.

My name is Kim Andy, and this is my story.

I am the mother of 3 boys (Jake, Josh, and Alex) and one stepdaughter (Sami). I live in South Williamsport, PA with my fiancé Steve. Together we learned that blended families can be difficult at times, but we did our best to make things work, to show our kids that they were loved, and that family comes in many different shapes and sizes.

My son Joshua struggled with anger, depression, and mood swings following my divorce from his dad. One day, when he was eight years old and had gotten into trouble, I heard him scream from his bedroom that he wished he was dead. In that moment my heart stopped, and I had the first panic attack of my life. Between all the different therapies, outpatient and inpatient care, issues at school and home, life became overwhelming and a daily struggle. In hindsight, I realize that I was so invested in helping Josh for so many years that I was not as "there" for my other children, or Steve, as much as I thought I was or should have been. I live with this guilt every day of my life.

Josh was eventually diagnosed with Oppositional Defiant Disorder. Our family went through years of extreme difficulty and chaos. It was an intense roller coaster ride that never seemed to end. One day Josh would be the sweetest kid in the world who would do anything for anybody. The next he would be angry, depressed and mean. We never knew which "Josh" we were going to have on any given day. We did everything we knew how at the time, as a family, to cope. During this time, I was also diagnosed with Multiple Sclerosis, Complex Migraines, Generalized Anxiety Disorder, and Major Depressive Disorder. It was a long, hard road, one where at times, I was not sure I, or my family, would make it through.

Fast forward to 2011/2012. The kids were all growing up. Josh was doing well and on a new path. He started going to youth group and church. After all the years of struggling, we were building a solid relationship and things were looking up. Life was good.

The day that changed everything

March 7, 2012 – I was driving down the highway coming home from picking up my prescription for pneumonia when I got the call. Josh was dead. He was in a single car accident and died on impact.

My mind could not comprehend those words and I started thinking so many thoughts all at the same exact time.

"Dead???"

"No."

"This is a mistake."

"I need to go see Josh"

"I can't, he is dead"

"Damn-it Josh, I told you to be careful driving!"

"Wait until I see you again, we are going to have a talk!"

"Wait, I won't see him again, he is dead."

"Oh my God my baby is dead!"

"I need to call Steve, the boys, Sami, but I need to get to the hospital. Wait... he is dead."

Journal Entry- March 10, 2012

I don't know how I am doing this Josh. I don't know how I am going on. It's not real, but of course it is. I don't know what to do. I can't think too much. Beyond this one moment in time. I don't know how I am going to do the viewing and funeral, tomorrow and Monday. God Joshy, I honest to God don't think I can. I just want to curl up in a ball. Every time someone says can I get you anything I want to cry out and say my son...

Somehow, I got through the viewing and the funeral. That first year I walked around in a thick, heavy fog. I learned early on to wear a mask while in public because grief scares people. I got so tired of putting that fake smile on my face just to please everybody else. That mask gets so heavy and uncomfortable. Why do I have to make everybody else feel better? Don't they know my son died? Inside I was screaming while on the outside I was smiling. People's perceptions of how I should feel, or act, wore on me. I wanted to scream whatever you imagine this to feel like, multiply that by a million. I felt like I was the best actress in the world. I swear I should have won an academy award.

The world was moving on as I remained in limbo. I felt torn between the past and the present, caught between two worlds. Which one could I possibly live in completely? I never realized that time itself could be so meaningless. I was unsure of what to do, unsure of my role, unsure of who I even was. I felt like an outsider, like I did not belong. I was stuck in a time warp, alone in this world yet not alone, wondering what the point of it all was. I felt abandoned, like I was drowning in my grief. I was the walking truth of what could happen at any given moment. Nighttime was the worst; I wanted all thoughts and feelings to cease. I didn't want to think, feel, or remember. I felt like I was a robot going through life.

The next months and years were a complete physical, emotional, and mental roller coaster ride. There were days when I just wanted to throw the covers over my head and say I lost this fight. I wanted to be weak. Why do people keep saying I am strong, I am amazing, I am such an inspiration? I felt like none of those things. I wanted to punch the wall. I wanted to scream at the top of my lungs. I wanted to wipe that stupid fake smile off my face. Just for that day. Then I would go back to being strong.

Then there were days where one moment I felt like I was dealing with things, the next I felt like my heart was being ripped from my chest. One day I was coping, the next I was going insane with the hurt. There were moments in time when reality would sock me right in the gut, and in an instant my heart felt like it weighed a ton and was being crushed by some kind of vise. I did not want to belong to this club anymore. I just wanted my son back and for my world to right itself again. How could I feel so lonely and trapped within my own feelings when I had so many people who loved me and were there for me? I couldn't express how I truly felt. I could not put it into words. Maybe I was afraid too, afraid people could not handle the truth, that their worlds were fragile and at any moment could change.

I sank into a deep, dark depression quite a few times over the years. Every time I fell into that deep, dark pit it would be harder and harder to pull myself out. Maybe one day I wouldn't. Life was a daily struggle and I missed Josh so much it hurt. I started questioning life and my purpose to the point I felt as if I was going to go insane. How do you lose a child and go on? After all we had been through, for him to be doing so well, and then he is just gone? Why?

I tried so hard to be strong, not drag others down with my grief. I always wore that mask so others could feel comfortable around me, regardless of how I was feeling. It seemed I couldn't do grief right. I grieved too much or too little. I was depressed, I needed to get out. The roller coaster ride seemed to have steeper hills, more turns, going faster and faster and I felt it was never going to stop. I couldn't keep pretending, even on my good days I couldn't keep my mask in place. I couldn't keep holding it all in. I was going to explode.

My motto became "**Just Twenty-Four More Hours.**" I would say this over and over sitting on my bed, rocking back and forth, holding a bottle of pills and a razor blade. Give it twenty-four more hours. This is the only thing that pulled me through. I would give it twenty-four more hours. The pain was so intense, I held it in for so long, that I turned to cutting. At the time I didn't even realize why I was doing it. I just knew in that moment; I felt a tiny bit of relief. I didn't really want to die. I just didn't want to be here. I wanted to disappear. I wanted to go to see Josh. But then I would have to leave Steve and the kids, and I couldn't do that. My love for them is just as strong as my love for Josh. I felt so torn. I was struggling to be strong in the presence of everybody else and then going home and taking off that heavy, disgusting mask and falling apart. Totally letting the hurt, anger and grief work its way through my body, heart, mind, and soul. It would rip me to shreds. I didn't know who to turn to. Everybody says they are there, but when you show the deep emotions of true, raw grief their reactions were usually to placate me or to threaten to call 911. I felt like I was living two lives. One where I was being who everybody wanted me to be and one where I was being my true self. It would have been so much easier to give up. To let the grief and despair take hold and just shut out the world.

I knew something had to give. I reached deep down inside to figure out what I wanted out of life. Did I want to use what I have been through and help others, or did I want to crawl in a hole and become angry and bitter? I had a choice. I know Josh is with me and that he is in the best place there is to be. I know that love never dies. What does Josh think when he sees me in total despair not living my life? I went to his grave and had a long talk with him and I made him a promise. I would use what he taught me to help others.

I started to change my thought process. I started to reach out to people, smile more, and practice gratitude. I have felt for a long time that there was something I should be doing, a purpose for all this. When I am helping others, I feel alive and passionate. I will forever miss Josh, but I know that he is more alive now than he ever was. I realized I can incorporate a new way of life, a new relationship, where I carry him with me every second of every day. I will have bad days, days I throw the covers over my head and don't get out of bed. But I will get back up. I will live my life to serve others and I will let go and let God lead the way of what I am on this earth to do. I realize that to heal properly I need to feel. I'm afraid to feel sometimes but there is no way around grief, I must go through it. I need to feel my feelings and then release them.

I vowed to make it my life mission to help those who feel hopeless and lost, to use my personal tragedy and make a difference in the lives of others. I have been to my lowest point where I felt like I would rather die than feel that deep squeezing pain anymore. It is okay to feel however you feel. To say this is my pain and I feel it and I own it. I took my power back.

One thing such a devastating loss has taught me is that I am truly grateful for what is important in life.

I am a new me. I love who I am and how much I have grown. I love that I can look at my life and everything that has happened and understand that it really is all for a reason, even though I may not understand it. I can find the good even through the bad. When I struggle, I realize that it is okay, it is okay to not be okay sometimes. I now realize that it is not the situation that determines our path. It is how we choose to look at it, respond to it, and how we can eventually apply that to our lives as we move forward. I am choosing to grow from this instead of becoming angry and bitter. This is certainly not an overnight process.

This is my new normal and I have embraced and accepted that. I have faith there is something greater out there and this journey we are on is only the beginning. I pray for strength daily, to be a better person, to make a difference. Love is what matters, for it transcends all, even death. Josh is with me for every step of my journey.

Although this has been the hardest, darkest thing I have ever been through, it has taught me the most about life. Loss has the power to reshape you from deep within - to mold you into either a person full of bitterness and hate or one of love and compassion. Through our struggles we gain so much strength and wisdom if we allow it.

When life seems impossible, I think of Josh alive and how spirited and full of life he was. How he was not afraid to die because he knew he was going to a better place. How he lived his life to the fullest. So, for now I understand I must do that too.

I carry Josh in my heart every day. Love does not die when the physical form dies. Love is always present, always with us.

About Kim Andy

 Kim Andy lives in South Williamsport, Pennsylvania with her Fiancé Steve, son Alex, and the beloved family dog, Lily. She works at STEP Inc., a Community Action Agency, where she has been able to use the multiple positions, she has held to reach out to those in need. By working alongside partnering agencies in the community, she uses her knowledge and understanding to help those in need to connect to resources that will aid them in their goal of attaining self-sufficiency. She has a passion for helping others, and since the loss of her 19-year-old son Joshua, has reached out to others with similar struggles to let them know they are not alone. "Just Twenty-Four More Hours" is Ms. Andy's first published work, although she has done extensive journaling in not only her private journals, but also on social media sites. Readers have encouraged her to start a blog or to write a book. It is her dream to use the knowledge she has gained throughout her life to give hope to those who feel they have none. Through tragedy and loss, she has now found her purpose. She plans to continue writing and to help others by facilitating a grief support group.

Connect with Kim Andy at:

www.just24morehours.com
https://www.facebook.com/dontlosehopeXOXO/
kim@just24morehours.com

Betrayed & Back: Pain To Purpose

By: Karen Prescod

When I think about the journey of my life, I reflect on the unexpected turns it took that led me from the despair and darkness of pain to the height, light, and triumph of purpose. A few years ago, I had neck surgery, and it put me in a debilitating situation that left me unable to walk and in chronic pain. Being fiercely independent before the surgery, I became dependent on other people.

How could I, a former champion athlete and model, successful corporate professional and entrepreneur, be the same person now depending on others to help me achieve the most basic needs? Laying down, sitting up, going to the bathroom, taking a shower, and walking. Things I took for granted before. I later realized my life had been training me for this moment. Everything I worked for, dreamed about, experienced, learned and encountered became the foundation I needed to grow from Pain to Purpose.

I grew up running, jumping, climbing and swimming in my native country of Trinidad & Tobago. I roamed and explored with an unending curiosity and a fearless excitement about experiencing my next new adventure. By nature, I want to understand how, and why things work. That curiosity extends to people - our minds, bodies and behavior. I observe, I study, I ask. Taking things apart, just to answer the questions of how and why. I am fascinated and amazed by patterns, sequences, routines, and order. The essence of who I am is built on identifying challenges, isolating the pieces, and finding solutions not only to overcome them but to use the knowledge gained to thrive and excel.

Figuring out what was happening to my body, understanding where the pain was coming from, how to eliminate it, and why it was happening, became my next new adventure. It began in my twenties, the unexplainable pain. At the time I would characterize it as discomfort, consistently uncomfortable aches, and numbness, that I dismissed. Headaches, shoulder pain, arm pain, neck pain and blurred vision. At home, work, friends, family, loved ones were all exposed to the side effects. Snappy, irritable, grumpy, short-tempered. Let's just say, I wasn't pleasant to be around. Finally, in 2000, I went in to see a doctor hoping to figure out what was wrong. I wish I could say that after the first visit I had a diagnosis, but I can't. It wasn't until 2003, that I found a doctor who had some answers and remedies to relieve my pain. I came out of my first surgery having vertebrae 4 and 5 fused, eventually feeling somewhat like my old self. I wasn't completely pain free, but it was nothing compared to what it was prior, it was at worst, tolerable and at best manageable. I was happy and thankful that I had some answers, some relief. I even enjoyed some perspective on my life and health. All my experiences and choices led me exactly where I needed to be.

By March 2009, the shooting electrical pain had me in its grip, and was worse than the pain I experienced before. Crippling, severe pain that began to affect my mobility. I could barely move my hand; my right arm was in a sling tight to my chest to keep it stationary because any movement caused pain in my neck. Eventually it was so debilitating that I could no longer work. I found myself back at the doctor's office, getting prescriptions for more pills, referrals for more MRI's, and more hours of physical therapy. All the same remedies, with the same result. NO RELIEF.

The morning of May 21st, 2009, I slowly walked into the hospital for surgery. My thoughts were vast, but they boiled down to one common thought – How did people live with chronic pain?

I didn't know or think at the time it would be my journey. I woke up after surgery in ICU with blood pressure that was out of control. They were trying everything to get it to drop, no matter what they did it didn't work. After being stabilized, I was moved to another room to recover. My right hand was weaker than my left, my right leg was attached to my body, but I couldn't use it, and my body had accepted the jobs of being both betrayer and teacher.

I was in a neck brace, the entire right side of my body had limited or no function, and I was having numbness, tingling, burning pain. Every different type of pain you can think of I was having it. I went back a week later for my first checkup, and it was then that we all realized I couldn't walk, and my daily routine to recover would consume my life.

Each day was filled with orthopedic and physical therapy for my body, but the physical pain was just the beginning. I often questioned if the pain was real, or if I was making it up. It was like having sensory overload. Physical, mental, emotional pain around everything was overwhelming. For some time, I was ok and hadn't really accepted that my life was changing. When I finally saw it, felt it, connected and accepted it, it spun into a cycle of depression that consumed me and almost destroyed my life. I developed anxiety, began to have severe panic attacks so bad that I was gasping for air, and felt like I was being stifled, drowned in my own water. It happened so fast that I didn't even know I was depressed. I was in denial. I remember a doctor asking me if I was depressed. I said no, without any doubt or hesitation. He then said to me that it would be hard not to be depressed with what I was dealing with. I listened, but I just didn't see it. He offered me some medication to help me through the process, I declined. By the 2nd or 3rd visit, I realized that maybe I was heading into a state of depression. That visit happened weeks before I attempted to take my life.

My days started with an interruption from sleep. Severe pain, it interrupted every aspect of my life. I slept on and off all day everyday due to the heavy amounts of medication. I was so "doped up" that I fell asleep while eating. I felt like a drug addict, every day the same routine. An hour just to get off the bed to use the bathroom or do anything. It was tough to move and even when I wanted to, I didn't have the energy to do it. It was a challenge even with a walker. For months I slept sitting up. Trying to get as comfortable as I could, but nothing was comfortable, nothing made sense. My body was consumed by the pain, but my mind and spirit

98

were consumed by despair, sorrow and hopelessness. Day after day, the darkness slowly enveloped me.

Depending on other people to bathe me, prepare my meals, support me financially, take care of me, was not who I was, but it was who I had become. Sitting in a chair taking up air and space, just existing, a life with no purpose.

There I was in a body that had betrayed me, in a relationship that was disintegrating under the weight of this new reality, depressed, consumed by pain, with thoughts of only one way out. I begged for just one minute, one minute that I was free from the pain. One minute that my body was released from the prison of burning, stabbing, pinching, pressure-filled all-consuming pain. I didn't want to suffer or hurt anymore. I reached for my blood pressure pills. I had just gotten 6 bottles refilled. One bottle at a time, I opened them, and handful by handful, I tossed them into my mouth to swallow my pain and drown my sorrow. In my mind, it would lower my blood pressure so low that I would leave this earth peacefully. That would be it, no more pain, I WOULD BE FREE. I just wanted to stop hurting and suffering, so I closed my eyes and gently and quietly drifted off to sleep. Bye, bye, perfectly planned.

But I woke up. From the moment I realized I survived; I knew the universe (God) had a greater purpose for me. Doctors could not believe I was alive. Nor could I.

In sitting in the realization and knowing, of that, I asked God to show me the way. Because I had attempted to end my life, I was committed to the psych ward for 13 days. Mandatory 3 days under the Baker Act and 10 additional days because of the severity of what I did. Which was worse the pain, or the psych ward? For days all I did was cry I didn't belong in there and I cried some more. One day a nurse came to me and said, "If you want to get out of here, you need to attend the group meetings." He encouraged me to go watch TV in the group room, because that was the only way to go home. I was good at using the rules to get what I wanted. I was good at adapting, and again I pretended to be doing better, but I was ANGRY. I was angry at everyone, including God. "Why did he do this to me?", I asked. "Why? What had I done so bad and wrong that I would get punished like this?" I was angry at God for a while. I began my journey back. I had to learn to walk again. I had to learn to trust again. I had to learn to hope again. And I did all those things. It wasn't easy, fast, or without setbacks. I chose me. I knew my body; I knew myself and more than anything I trusted that I had support greater than me and the doctors. I realized in my walk back from betrayal that God had not punished me, and that my life wasn't over. One of me did die, but it was the version of myself that lived a life that wasn't authentic or aligned with my purpose. My true life was just beginning.

When I arrived in Fort Lauderdale, FL in September 2011, I had a plan. Once again, the plan that I had for myself, was not the plan that the universe, God had for me. I ended up alone, with no place to live. For three weeks I was homeless and lived in my car. Looking back and reflecting on that time, it was one of the happiest times in my life. I would spend from 5:00 am to 11:00 pm on the beach, meditating, sleeping, people watching, swimming, thinking and listening. It was liberating, nowhere to be, no one to answer to, just being and experiencing life. By January I found a spiritual center and started attending services. It was another way for me to take care of myself. It allowed me to understand and accept that there is a reason that people come into our lives and it taught me to truly forgive and let go. Forgiveness is a powerful action and meaningful process. It is true that it isn't for those being forgiven, but for those forgiving. I discovered peace, created space in my heart, healed my body and opened myself up to hear the quiet whispers of truth and purpose when I was able to forgive.

I had been getting messages about my purpose for years before I sat and listened to hear them. They began as quiet whispers, busy like the buzzing of a bumble bee as it zips closely by your ears in the heat of the summer. I often thought that the whispers got louder, but the truth of the matter is that I listened closer. "Create a non-profit for kids", the voice would whisper over and over. Surrendering instead of resisting was also another valuable lesson that my journey had gifted to me. When I surrendered myself to that truth, I was empowered to seek answers and ask questions. "What kids would I help? Who would they be?", I'd ask.

In 2013 the whisper shared its secret. It revealed my purpose and honored me with the answer. I had traveled my journey not for me, not as punishment or even glory. I had traveled to be in service to others, to children. My purpose was to create an organization to help children impacted by chronic pain. I was chosen to travel my journey to lay the foundation for a nonprofit, Bowtie Kids – Courage and Confidence for Kids with Chronic Pain. My questions, my journey of chronic pain, my walk into darkness, led me to purpose. I couldn't see before what was right in front of me and many times, in life we don't. Life is a beautiful teacher. She is a mysterious giver, who is honest, connected and committed to who we truly are. She makes no mistakes, is fluid like the ocean and solid like the earth when we need her to be so that she can honor us with gifts of love. I am here to share my story with you as a reflection of her greatness. With hope, all is possible. Our journey in life is meant to free us from who we think we are and reveal to us the beauty of who we were born to be. I believed that I was betrayed by my body, my perception, my past, I was even betrayed by myself. The truth is that I was given gifts that I used along my path to lead me back to my purpose. It was the path, my only path that I needed and chose to grow from pain to purpose. Each of us has a path.

What are your whispers revealing to you?

Who are you, and where are you going?

Life is whispering are you ready to listen?

When we listen, answers come, and we find that the path was exactly what it needed to be.

I want to leave you with a few takeaways that you may find useful. There are many valuable lessons in life, but only few that shape the foundation where the others will reside;

1.) Everything is temporary. In the midst of my darkest moments, I didn't believe there was light at the end of the tunnel, let alone a brighter side. Remember that nothing lasts forever, so remain committed to your goal, and don't get consumed by your feelings, they are fleeting;

2.) Truth and transparency are liberating. When you know who you are, you have the power and authority to authentically express your truth with a freedom that allows you to soar like an eagle; and

3.) Your story is valuable, be powerful, share freely. You are a light of inspiration, be a beacon for another. Be Relentless. Be Resilient. Be Empowered. Be Confident. Be Courageous.

About Karen Prescod

Karen Prescod aka The Bowtie Gurl Bio

 Karen Prescod is an empowerment agent who believes in our ability to harness and utilize the power of our minds and knowledge, to create a life of truth and authentic expression. She is the Founder and Chief Statement Maker of The Bowtie Gurl ™ - Empowering Women to Challenge the Stereotype of Traditional Fashion, and the Visionary and Founder of Bowtie Kids™ - Courage & Confidence For Kids With Chronic Pain. Both her business and non-profit are built on the foundation of 5 Empowerment Principles. Self-Discovery, Self-Awareness, Self-Worth, Self-Expression, Social Engagement & Advocacy. She has served on the board of directors for the Greater Fort Lauderdale Chamber of Commerce, the Executive Committee, Government Affairs Committee, Nominating Committee, Gay and Lesbian Business Exchange (GLBX) Council, where she is a past chair, and the Women's Council where she is the immediate past chair. She was also awarded the 2016 Chair's Award (which is presented to the chair that has the most impact in the community). Honored as one of Fort Lauderdale's Most Powerful Women, by Gold Coast Media Group, Karen has been highlighted and featured in multiple media campaigns as a friend and advocate for a variety of groups and organizations, represented in the diverse Fort Lauderdale community. Karen is a sought-after empowerment

speaker and moderator. She is a powerful, confident, loving woman whose vision for the world is oneness. To learn about what she is creating in the world, visit KarenPrescod.com, TheBowtieGurl.com, BowtieKids.org, or engage personally with Karen at karen@karenprescod.com.

SHATTERPROOF

In the eye of the storm

By: Nancy Beer

It was early April and I had a four-day weekend coming up, to fly across country to my youngest son Christopher's home in Colorado and meet my granddaughter on her first birthday. As I prepared to get in the car for the two-hour drive to the airport, my phone rang, it was my oldest son AJ's wife Beth and she was frantically crying. They needed money again, as usual there was an emergency, pulling on my heartstrings this time it was for a prescription for the baby's diaper rash. Maddox my five-month-old grandsons diaper rash was so bad it was bleeding Beth cried out; your trip isn't as important. I stated that I recently sent funds and they have Medicaid it would pay for any medications needed. All the money I had was for my trip and my other family members who are important too. I'd spent so much time, effort and funds over the years on my oldest son that I almost felt negligent when it came to the rest of the family. As I drove, I began to feel guilty, what if it was true and this new medicine wasn't covered? Should I cancel my trip and drive the five hours to help my grandson? I called back and spoke to AJ; he didn't have a clue what I was talking about. All I could think was what do you mean, you don't know, since he was the one that normally did the feeding, bathing and such for the kids? I didn't have time or the will to call anyone out on a lie for money again, so I sent $40. It was just easier to give in so that I could get on with the adventure that I had planned, an enabling trait I'd picked up over the years that you could call a desperation decision.

I was very excited about this trip and determined to be joyful, when I arrived in Denver, I was greeted by my son Chris and grandson Christopher. This was going to be a wonderful long weekend; smiles, hugs, bedtime stories, cherished moments. These three grandchildren didn't really know me that well, only over the phone and stories from daddy. My dream was to fly out every three months and things were looking up financially, so this was to be the start of a new family bonding experience. Little did we know that our whole world was about to change.

Thursday and Friday were great we had a lot of fun. Late Friday night I received a social media message from Beth, stating that AJ didn't know who she was, and they were considering taking him to the hospital assuming that his liver was failing and would keep me updated. I tried calling for two hours straight but no answer, I called all of the local hospitals he wasn't there. Here I was a whole day and a half drive away and I felt helpless. You see my oldest son and his wife were battling opioid addiction, six months earlier, AJ had gotten clean and sober and had bright new plans. Then slide back when he and his wife, who at the time was pregnant, moved to help her family member. I got down on my knees and prayed, I can't help this time Heavenly Father, it has to be You! After praying with everything I had and no more tears came I felt a supernatural peace and although I still knew something definitely was not OK with whatever was happening over on the East Coast with my firstborn while I was out west, that the most powerful force in the universe has His hands in it, and I could lay down and rest.

The next morning, I told Chris that we needed to be in prayer for his brother, perhaps since we hadn't heard anything then no news was good news. Chris wondered and rightly so if they were just crying wolf with a plan for getting more money, anything is possible when dealing with the madness of another's addiction. This I knew to be true as I had lived with and around addiction most of my life though this time felt intuitively real. I tried my best to be in the moment with the children but fear kept creeping in, I couldn't get through the feeling of dark, soul consuming anger to pray so I went for a walk and called the 700 club Prayer Line that I have been using for many years and again was comforted and the burden lightened. It was Saturday and the last full day to spend with my loves in Colorado. We would go back and forth between moments of peace, playing with the kids while trying to contact AJ. Finally, I received a text from Beth saying yes, it was his liver and they gave him charcoal he's OK but throwing up everywhere. They still wouldn't answer the phone, three hours later another Facebook message came through saying "AJ can't walk, or talk, doesn't know any of us and I can't deal with this!" After 10 straight calls in a row, wondering if his heart still beats, someone picked up the phone screaming "I'm not talking to her, here AJ" apparently shoving the phone at him. I said "AJ?" He answered "yeah" then after that nothing made sense it was all just muffled nonsense. I begged them

108

to call 911 but the answer was, they couldn't have authorities coming there because of drugs in the house. I implored, "Drag him outside, then they won't have to come in!" I called 911 myself and figured OK I'll be home late Sunday night; they will help till I can get to him.

Sunday morning came and I assumed I could just call the hospital and find out he's OK, none of the local hospitals had him listed as a patient, oh no not again! Calling and calling I finally got an answer and we were told that AJ refused to go with the ambulance but still could not walk or talk, how could a person in his state refuse? Points of rage growled at Beth "If he dies, I'm coming for you" as if the whole of what his addiction brought into our family over the years was her fault. I told her no more, you will take him NOW or I will call the police, she reluctantly agreed. There was just a few hours left till I had to get on the plane, this may sound strange but I felt released to bring in others, so I called my husband Roger for prayer, then my father, AJ's father and a cousin, told them what was going on and asked them to go to the hospital to meet them there? Now with a half an hour to go before the two-hour flight then my layover I received a call from my dad saying they've been waiting, and AJ isn't there. I called Beth, they had been sitting in the parking lot the whole time, searching the Internet about what they can do to make him come out of this trip that he was stuck in. I just knew that it was time, so I hung up the phone and called the police described the car, occupants and place. Surrounded by an airport full of people I desperately blasted out, "My son was in the car and he is dying but the people he's with will not let him out!" Just 10 minutes before takeoff the hospital security officers found them as they were preparing to pull out, they surrounded the car, opened the door and picked up my son and carried him into the emergency room like a ragdoll. Dad called me saying they saw him, and everyone is praying.

Not knowing what was happening to my son except that he was in good hands and God was there, I got on my plane and again was enveloped in waves of peace and slept. Upon landing I turned airplane mode off and immediately received multiple messages telling me that AJ had suffered a massive hemorrhagic stroke and is in a medically induced coma until they can get him stable. I was to call the social worker immediately to arrange to make medical power of attorney decisions and that his dad was holding the role until I arrived. With a three-hour layover and this news, I was stunned, how does one act in this type of experience, I didn't know. What I thought I knew, it was crumbling into a heap of fear and dread on the floor, wasn't it? As I stumbled through the airport, heartbroken and alone, I heard a voice standing out above all others, it sounded far away and at that moment I knew, I had to get to that man. Think a preacher voice, southern accent, authoritarian yet comforting, and it belonged to a tall man talking on his phone. I walked right up to him with tears in my eyes and trembling in my voice I stated, "My son has suffered a massive hemorrhagic stroke from a drug overdose can you pray with me?" "Yes, dear one" he said. As he began to pray, I watched people continue to join us, it

110

was unbelievable the amount of people who surrounded us. God had sent me an army. His voice was loud, commanding and loving all at the same time it left no room for anything other than faith and belief in something BIGGER than us, right here right now!

As it turned out our two-hour layover changed to a cancellation due to a mechanical issue, the airline was to put us up in a hotel. As we stood in line to make arrangements for the next day flight, I received the news that I wouldn't be able to fly home until late the next night, this was not acceptable I told the agent, my son has just had a stroke and I can't stay here I must go to him. A gentleman tapped me on the shoulder, turns out he was an ambassador from another country heading into Washington DC for an important meeting and he asked if he could bless me with his first-class ticket out on the early flight and he would take mine. God just kept sending people to comfort and assure me of His presence.

My husband Roger shared that he spent much time in prayer and had a supernatural confirmation of peace as well. Upon arriving at our home to pick up him and AJs oldest three children then drive the five hours to be with their dad, I saw that a flower I've kept in my home even though it hadn't bloomed for 3 years was completely full of blooms even on many new stalks. This is exactly what they mean by, "A God wink" and it gave me more strength to face this.

The children's mother did not want them to see their dad intubated and, in a coma, in case it was the last time. I was so torn, if it was the last chance to say bye daddy and I love you, how could

I take that away. I decided to deal with that bridge later, until then we had each child record a message on our phones to play for their daddy.

As it turned out, the peace I'd been given on Friday night was truth, God was in that mess with AJ the whole time, even throughout the fear and neglect of his fellow Addicts. You see, this hospital is a teaching university and the most knowledgeable neurologist for drug overdoses in the USA arrived on Sunday to tour the hospital before his lectures began on Monday. Had he not been there to confer with on Sunday, protocol would have left him with a very low survival rate and a high chance of him being a vegetable (what an awful word picture that is). It took 30 days to bring and keep the swelling in AJ's brain down. At first, he was like a kid, I remember thinking if it stays this way, maybe that's ok, at least he's happy, not bitter or angry or guilt laden anymore.

We are coming up on the 4th year anniversary of this overdose and new birth day, the fall out is daily damage control. AJ has brain damage, his central control center (thalamus) takes all signals and turns them into pain on the right side of his body. On a bad day, a nice breeze shows up to us, but to his right side as icy-fire, sending his muscles into spasms that will curl under his right foot.

AJ survived what most addicts do not, he left behind that life to focus on being the best father possible with his second chance.

There is a dark side to this human experience, addiction and its ravages on families, human exploitation in all its ugly forms, hate crimes and then there's the large numbers of suicide among our youth to name a few. How can one person make a difference, we share our stories of hope and triumph over adversity. We band together as Elite Foundation is doing, and the more we talk about these things, the more likely the hurting ones know we are here with our eyes and arms wide open.

This is what I know to be true from living through this experience. God had to take me halfway across the country because my son would choose on a Friday to shoot a lethal dose of drugs (that I paid for by sending that $40) in his arm and I would have immediately came to the rescue with only being a 5 hour drive away calling on our family to start the process. The neurologist whose knowledge and wisdom saved AJ's life would not have been there yet. All those people that The Creator sent to me would not have had the experience of connecting in another soul's time of need.

Even right there in the eye of the storm, in the valley of the shadow of death, walking hand in hand with the madness of heroin addiction; faith was my shield. The peace that I had been given was not a feeling but a PLACE to wait in the light. I am grateful to have already been in tune with God's presence so that I recognized it as louder than the darkness of despair. No matter what anyone says, I know without a doubt that faith is a not a weakness rather it is strength, not just in your time of need but every second of your life.

I survived; I get to LIVE in my future. AJ

Are we humans shatterproof?

No, we are not, but in the living of this terrifying yet miraculous experience my faith in God remains SHATTERPROOF.

About Nancy Beer

Nancy Beer is an International Bestselling author, entrepreneur, runway model, literary agent, healthcare professional, caregiver, case manager and Certified Genotype Change Coach for her oldest son who is a hemorrhagic stroke survivor due to a drug overdose.

Nancy grew up in rural West Virginia and wants you to know that Forest Therapy really is a thing.

A sought-after speaker and storyteller with a passion for creating less vulnerable people in our world, healing to the hurting and HOPE! Currently she is advocating for free self-defense and situational awareness classes in her area and yours within the USA.

Nancy's fascination of the power of plants and how in the right combination can bring health to us, led her to a home-based business called Lifevantage. Protandim is a Nrf2 activator and can drop your oxidative stress by 40% (which is at the center of 300 disease processes) with 12 patents and 23 peer reviewed studies on Pubmed.com (where doctors go for research). Research it for yourself on Pubmed, type in Nrf2 and your illness then contact Nancy to learn how you can Biohack your aging code with this plant combination.

Nancy lives in Virginia with her husband Roger, they have 3 fur babies, 3 adult children and 10 grandkids. Roger and Nancy enjoy riding his motorcycle and are members of a motorcycle ministry called Honorbound.

To connect with Nancy Beer:

Facebook.com/Nancy.s.Beer

Facebook.com/NancyBeerinbloom

Email: nancycanhelp@yahoo.com

www.NancyBeer.lifevantage.com

The Gift of Forgiveness

By: Nicole Harvick

If you don't love yourself, nobody will. Not only that, you won't
be good at loving anyone else. Loving starts with the self.

~Dr Wayne Dyer

Five years ago I would not have not even noticed this simple
quote much less understood the deep meaning.
I would have never imagined the power this simple quote has
given me.
I could have never imagined that this quote would change my life.
Learning to love myself has been my catalyst for practicing
kindness, compassion and finally understanding the basic need that
all humans have, it is to be loved and accepted for who we are.

A world without Hope,
A seeker not knowing what to seek, A darkness without light,
Why am I empty and what will fulfill me?
I had so many questions with despair seemingly the only answer.
My mind was screaming at me that I was doing everything wrong.
A mother first and a wife last, or so I was told.
My husband was cheating on me and had been for quite some
time.
Six years of his journaling that I read in stunned disbelief detailing
how he felt about me. The words were shocking and very painful.
After 20 years of marriage, I felt like I had been punched in the

stomach.

I now had a very important question to ask myself, who am I and what am I looking for?

Where should I start?

What now?

Dear 2013, I hate you!!

Slowly, I came to accept my new reality.

After 20 years of being married, I am getting a divorce.

I am selling my home of 14 years.

I am on my own.

Having been forced into a sequestered silence for so many years, I now wanted to scream at the top of my lungs. I wanted to lash out at my husband and the women he slept with.

My only emotion seemed to be fear, coupled with anger and rage.

I was starting to become physically ill.

I had migraines. I would scratch at my skin until I was bruised and sometimes bleeding. My hair was thinning.

I needed help and I needed it quick!

I started going to counselors but all they seemed to have me do is rehash the events of the past which only allowed all of the pain to resurface again and again.

I went to support groups only to find more rehashing of the events but now with added negativity.

I confided in friends and that always seemed to culminate with the same ending of reliving the pain and much unwanted advice.

Having always been interested in the meta-physical world, it was there that I started to re-explore. The books came first. I devoured and digested everything I could on self-help thru meditation. I studied cellular memory and explored the path of letting go thru past life regression. I read everything I could on mindfulness. I chanted mantras and used mudras. The classes came next. I became a Reiki Master, I took classes and became certified in Energy Healing, I also became certified in Sound Therapy. All of this was incredibly helpful to me and is still to this day. Something was still missing.

As it turned out, that something was forgiveness.

In the fall of 2014, I was eagerly anticipating a trip to the Island of Hawaii. I have always had a love affair with this magical place. I had moved to Oahu right after High School at the age of 17. The minute I stepped off the plane, I felt different. The Island breeze was soothing, and the colors were bright and vivid. You feel as if the Island wraps its arms around you and embraces you. It felt like home.

I was very excited to begin my journey back there. I meditated daily and at the time, I had no idea how important this particular meditation was going to be. As I listened closely, I heard my guides tell me to feed the stray. I assumed the stray to be a dog. When we finally reached our destination, I started casually looking for a dog that might need a handout. As the trip progressed, I put the thought in the back of my mind.

Several days into our visit, we decided to hike the Kilauea Volcano. This is an amazing hike which show cases the natural beauty of the island. It is lush, green and dense. It is also full of beautiful wildlife. We had hiked several miles and came upon a rope bridge. I noticed a deep ravine underneath us. It was there that I once again heard the voice of my guides speaking to me. They told me I was to make an offering to the island. I had purchased two maple bars prior to our hike and I now threw one into the ravine. I was also told to give thanks to the island for allowing me to be a part of such beauty and serenity. As we continued to hike down the trail, I stopped for a moment and just listened. It was at that moment that I heard a loud rustling noise, as I looked to see where the sound was coming from, I noticed deep in the foliage, a small hobbled bird. I had found the stray!

My daughter then bent down to feed to feed the bird the remaining maple bar. It ate right from her hand.

It was upon my return home that I noticed something strange. I kept seeing and hearing the word Ho'oponopono. It came up in conversations, and I kept seeing it in print. It was as if someone was sending me a message. I can now say that I will be forever grateful that I paid attention and listened to what that message was.

Having never heard of this, I thought the best way to start would be to educate myself on what this strange looking word was. I discovered that Ho'oponopono is an ancient Hawaiian Method of

Forgiveness.

I decided that maybe I should give it a try.

I had spent so much time and so much money on counselors, books and classes, it seemed doubtful something so simple could work. And it was free it must not be any good I reasoned. But at this point I had nothing to lose.

Again, I heard my guides, "Just Try It"

So, I did.

Ho'oponopono is very powerful and concise and consists of 4 phrases

I love you

I'm sorry

Please forgive me

Thank you

Ho'oponopono is about obtaining inner peace and harmony within yourself and with all mankind. The best English translation is "To Make Right"

Forgiveness can release us from the invisible chains that bind us. It can free us from the many burdens that we no longer wish to carry. Forgiveness is a healer. Forgiveness is the most important gift that we will ever give ourselves.

"The weak can never forgive

Forgiveness is the attribute of the strong"

~Mahatma Gandhi

I decided to start using Ho'oponopono daily. I used it over and over with pure intent.

I started by lying in a comfortable position in a quiet room. When I selected who I was working with, I used visualization to see that person.

- I envisioned my ex-husband. I thanked him for the two beautiful daughters he had given me.
- I thanked him for the life he had provided me by allowing me to be a stay at home mom and to raise my girls.

   I also forgave him for the many cruel words that had been exchanged over the years and I asked him to forgive me of the same.

   I told him I was sorry for the outcome of our relationship which ended in divorce.

   I sent him unconditional love, not as my husband but as a soul who not only needed but deserved love.

- I truly believe that love is our earthly lesson and it is the reason we are here on this planet.
- After I completed the forgiveness process, I chose to sever the energy chord that connected us. This is an

invisible cord that connects us to our higher self and to the people around us. In Hawaii, this is referred to as the Aca cord. Cutting cords is a simple process. To begin, you will want to be in a meditative state. Visualize the cord between you and the person you will be severing. When you have found the cord, decide where the cut should be made and then visualize the cord being cleanly severed. It is important to remember you are not cutting off the relationship you are just releasing energy that no longer serves you.

After completing the forgiveness process several times, something incredible started to happen. My tears of sorrow ceased to flow, I found myself having more energy. My inner doubt of who I was subsided, and where there had once existed anger, animosity and hate, there now existed love. And this love was different. This was a love that was deep and unconditional. And it was love for me!

This practice also led me to a very poignant epiphany. I realized I was not sad for what I had and lost, I was sad for what I thought I had and didn't.

This allowed me to truly understand my situation and it was the clarity I needed to continue my journey of healing.

It also taught me that the most important person to forgive is ALWAYS you. Blaming yourself for what you think are failures blocks your natural flow of love.

Try to remember there is no such thing as failure, there is only feedback.

Love should always flow thru us both easily and fluidly. Not just for our fellow humans but for all sentient creatures on Gods earth.

It was with these realizations that I allowed my heart to expel all the darkness and refill itself with the light of unconditional love. Once I learned to forgive, I realized that the forgiveness was for me. *For the first time, it allowed me to finally love myself. My world had shifted.*

It was thru love and forgiveness that I was led to this path with the desire to share my knowledge with as many people I can.

I have had many people tell me they are not ready to forgive the person they felt wronged them. If I could give one piece of advice, it would be this, do not do that to yourself. The only person who will suffer will be you. Do not carry the emotional baggage of someone that has wronged you. Love is much lighter than hate. Love yourself enough to free yourself from these chains that bind you.

To be of service and to facilitate healing is my greatest calling. I am beginning to incorporate Ho'oponopono into my Reiki practice. By merging these two great forces, we can not only begin to forgive, we can also move out the stagnant energies that build up in our bodies over time. Dark energies of negativity can be removed allowing powerful and positive energies to take their place. This creates a harmony within the body that allows you to raise your vibration and energy level.

I love and believe in this practice so much that I have started on a new path of creating bracelets, oils and candle's that will have the essence and scents that correlate with each of sayings. All of my products will be vibrationally infused with the magic of Reiki and blessed with love and abundance.

Ho'oponopono is my passion and it has become my way of life. I would encourage you to try this method of healing. It can't hurt anything but just think of what it can help. Of course, there will always be days when the ego rears its ugly head. I now know that it is just a part of this earthly life. I have learned how to deal with this and quickly release my stress, anger and my negative emotions.

I have learned many things thru this process of healing and enlightenment.
I have learned that the act of not forgiving a person only hurts you. It is like drinking poison and expecting the other person to die.

I have also learned that loving yourself first helps to illuminate the world around you. We are all connected so shine brightly and allow those with the same vibration to find you. It creates a better life not only for you but for those you surround yourself with. Be the example that others follow:

Love is the highest vibration there is in this universe. It is what we are sent here to learn. Help others to understand this.
Love is that which will always connects us to source.
Love is the answer to your every question.
Loving yourself allows you to become the best version of you!

I know that my journey with love and forgiveness will continue throughout my lifetime. With that said, I would like to thank you, the reader for allowing me to share my story. I send you much love and many blessings and hope that you too find your path to becoming Unstoppable!

About Nicole Harvick

 Nicole Harvick is the CFO of Don't "Diss" Abilities, an Arizona Non-Profit and 501c-3. Don't "Diss" Abilities was created to provide resources and activities for the handicapable community. Together with her daughter Madi, they co-wrote the children's book, "Boy on a Swing'. This book is the true story of how Madi became involved with her passion for helping individuals with disabilities.

Nicole is also very passionate about Ho'oponopono. It is this practice she credits for turning her life around. She is a Reiki Master and certified in Sound Therapy and Energy Healing. She is a lover of magic, moonlight, and mystery.

You can learn more about her at www.ofmanyworlds.com www.omnisourceblog.com and at Facebook under the name Spirit Talk. Nicole has two daughter's Madi 24 and Keely 16 and splits her time between Arizona and South Carolina

Facebook: Nicole Harvick
Instagram: nicole_harvick
Facebook Spirit Talk
www.ofmanyworlds.com
www.omnisourceblog.com

The Nameless Face

By: Debra Marsalisi

As I drive down Federal Highway the sun beats through the driver's side window. I try to avoid this area of town whenever possible. Over twenty years had passed since that day. I passed by the building where you raped me. The rapid flashes of memories fire across my mind like a scene from a bad movie. I realized then, I have absolutely no recollection of your name or even how we first met. I remember we only knew each other for a few days. At this point in my life you are a *Nameless Face* to me. The most instinctual response to the memory was to shove it back down even deeper. Raging denial surges through every fiber of my being. I think," It's no big deal" …, "it was quick" ⋯, "really, what did you expect; you went up to that abandoned floor with him?" ⋯… "NOOOO!" I cried out to the unwanted memory. That's when I hear your sweet, still voice Lord, inside my head and heart "Do you want to be whole?" I respond, "No, Lord PLEEEEASE not this", I don't want to deal with this, please anything but THIS!!"

Divine timing truly does exist; I would be attending a leadership and personal growth program that week. Little did I know I would participate in an exercise where I would be asked to share a painful memory. I sat facing a loving friend, our hands intertwined; she came to support me in the program. Her eyes were filled with compassion and warmth, she watched as I begin to squirm in my seat. I nervously adjust myself in a feeble attempt to get a little more comfortable. I was carefully scanning the room for the nearest exit. I desperately longed to bolt from the room. It is then I am struck with the reality that the drive the week early was to put me face to face with this memory. The prompting from the Holy Spirit began rising up in me…" Tell your story, Debra." A flush of heat surged through every fiber of my being; I began to shake. The heaviness on my chest made it difficult to breath. I had not uttered a word of the incident since the day it happened, not to another living soul. I sat there for what felt like an eternity. I closed my eyes; I attempted to take a slow, deep breath. My lips began to tremble, as I tried to form the word RAPE; my voice was practically inaudible….

Today, I write this letter to two individuals, my perpetrator and my younger self.

Nameless Face,

We only knew each other for a few days when you stopped by my office to see me on my lunch break. You suggested we go up to the fourth floor; there was an area in the building that was being renovated. It was empty; we could hang out and talk. I chose to go with you. I didn't know "talk" really meant rape. It all happened in a blink of an eye; within seconds of getting there, you had me firmly pressed against the wall, with my panties around my ankles, and were repeatedly thrusting yourself inside me. I was hit with an enormous wave of shock, disbelief, and numbness. I thought to

129

myself, is this really happening? Many sexual abuse survivors have one of three survivor responses, fight, flight or freeze. I froze. I could hardly get out that one syllable word NO that was running rampant through my brain. I liken it to a bad dream where you attempt to scream, but no words come out. Quit honestly, I'm unsure how long the violation lasted; it felt like it was happening in slow motion. When the word NO finally stammered out of my mouth, you eventually stopped. You said nothing, went on your way, never to be seen again. I pulled up my panties, straighten my clothes and hair, and I walked back into the office shell-shocked, as if nothing had happened. That day I chose to harden my heart.

Up until writing this letter I chose to wrap the memory of my frozen response in deep shame and anger. From a young age I was a girl teeming with rage that was my mask, my protective armor .... where was all that anger and rage when I actually needed it!? Where was all my fight? "Oh my wall, my wall.... if only I had built the bricks of my emotional wall higher maybe this never would've happened". I was comforting myself with convenient lies, self-soothing with denial. I determined the violation was just another moment in my timeline, which validated and fueled my deeply rooted feeling of insignificance, and worthlessness; feelings I had held onto like a bag of heavy rocks strapped across my crippled back, I had carried that bag since childhood.

I chose to suppress the memories and emotions as a way to survive; otherwise the painful lies of, "You deserved this, you went with him, what did you expect, you're nothing but a whore," would stream through my consciousness with a haunting cadence. Consistently subduing the memories and emotions caused me to become fiercely numb. On the outside I appeared strong and put together, but internally I was a shell of a person, I was the walking dead. Oh, how truly detached I was to get raped on my lunch hour, shake it off and go back to the office like nothing happened. I was emotionally crippled to stay silent for over twenty years.

I refuse to be angry with <u>myself</u> anymore. Twenty years is long enough!

Dear Younger Me,

No matter what <u>anyone</u> thinks or says you did NOT deserve this, please forgive yourself for freezing; it was a learned behavior from your early childhood sexual abuse. By the grace of God, today you have moved from victim to victor. You are more than a survivor, you're an overcomer, you're meant to thrive!

Younger me, please allow me the blessed opportunity to lovingly and tenderly minister to your sweet soul. Let me remind you of your true identity. Washing you in the Word of Truth, you are a beloved, beautiful daughter of the Most High God. His intimate knowledge of you is eternal. He has known you before the foundations of the earth. The Almighty has personally knitted you together in your mother's womb. He has washed you clean from your sins and the sins that others perpetrated on you.

Debra you have a divine purpose: You are God's workmanship that word in the original Greek is poiema, it's where we get the word poem, it's another way of saying you are His epic poem of Creation, His beautiful work of art. You have been hand-picked by the God of the Universe to bear good fruit, sweet girl. You bare good fruit when you help and love others going through similar pain. To weep with those who weep, and when their grieving is complete, help individuals find their true identity in Christ. The same God who created rich green valleys, deep blue oceans, rugged mountains, and the vast galaxies, looked at the world and thought the canvas of creation needed one of you too! WOW Little One, just wow! Please let that truth saturated your soul! Ephesians 2:10

Debra you are celebrated: The God of the Universe is delighted to sing over you. Oh, how precious is His unfailing love for you. Let the LORD's song of love and redemption cascade over you. Lift your hands high to heaven and feel the Abba's embrace. Zephaniah 3:17

Debra, you are completely understood and loved, more than you can possibly comprehend: Hebrews 4:15 teaches, Jesus understands suffering and shame. Nothing in all creation is hidden from His sight. Everything is uncovered and lay bare before Him. He truly understands your pain! Dear younger me, I believe Jesus is well acquainted with the shame of sexual abuse too. Artists throughout history have inaccurately painted pictures of His

132

crucifixion, suffering on the cross wrapped in a loin cloth. However, He was completely naked and exposed during the entire torturous event. Nakedness in the Hebrew culture carried with its great shame and humiliation. He was crucified naked in front of great crowds of screaming people. But He thought YOU were worth it, humanity was worth it; all the despair, affliction and shame were worth it...to reconcile you to God, to pay your sin debt, to wash you clean. YOU ARE worthy, YOU ARE significant. You do not have to live numb anymore; a loving and understanding God wants to walk you through the pain, so you can be healed and whole. So, your testimony can lead others to HIM.

Nameless Face,

Today I chose to boldly walk into forgiveness. Not because it's easy and CERTAINLY NOT because I believe what happen was okay. I am called to forgive as the Lord has forgiven me. See on the cross God's sacrificial love provided me with life affirming forgiveness I could not earn, and I did not deserve. I forgive you because God, through Christ forgave me of ALL my wickedness, depravity and rebellion. Through His blood He washes me clean. You see, the Author and Finisher of my faith has already woven redemption and forgiveness into the fabric of my story. I pray one day you seek HIS forgiveness. Forgiveness and salvation are available to all who will repent and believe.

I pray that one day you will surrender your life over to the Savior, so He may transform you into a man of honor and integrity.

I pray for the safety of the women in your life, the ones you love and cherish the most, such as your mother, sister, wife or daughter; that they will never have to endure a sexual violation. Not by your hands or anyone else's.

This day I choose to reclaim my freedom from these toxic beliefs and behavior patterns; I will NOT live numb or walk in deadness. I chose to rejoice in who God says I am. I am a picture of God's masterful creativity, His redemption, restoration, healing, transformation, and His Amazing Grace and you can be too.

"Forever wrapped in HIS Righteous Arms"

Debra

Thank you for spending time with me, as I shared my story. I believe my healing journey came in several stages; a voyage into the pain, resolution, genuine forgiveness and learning to walk in a new identity. In sharing, I hope to encourage others to rest in the realization they're not alone, trauma doesn't define or determine their destiny, and finally that life is an amazing adventure when one walks in healing and wholeness.

Voyage into the pain:

The first lesson I've learned is that numbing the pain was a prison cell designed by my own hands. Numbness looks different to different people, it can be in the form of denial to your feelings or it can be self-destructive behaviors, such as turning to substances to self-medicate. I now understand it's truly impossible to heal and

134

forgive until you allow yourself to feel the brunt of the pain. The prison cell of numbness was carefully crafted to avoid feeling pain, to avoid trust, but in all actuality, it prolonged my pain and kept me extremely guarded. If I'm not vigilant I can wander right back into that prison cell and shackle myself to the wall. It takes a constant effort not to use numbness as my go-to defense mechanism; to allow myself to feel, to be courageous enough to lovingly express my hurts and disappointments regardless of how uncomfortable that might be. And finally, to be brave enough to trust, to grant others the grace to make mistakes without tossing out relationships at the first sign of conflict. I am a work in progress, but I know I'm worth the effort.

Resolution:

I no longer choose to look back on my life with regret. I choose to look forward with a teachable heart so I may continue to learn from life's many challenges. I have willfully given up on the *"what ifs"* in life. *What if* I never experience sexual abuse as a little girl, *what if* I never endured a rape as a young woman? *What if* I hadn't had a string of unhealthy relationships? These *"what ifs"* were mental predators that stole and destroyed my emotional well-being; they robbed me of my joy. I chose to rejoice in my victories AND my trials. There's significance and purpose to suffering and I have learned to be a good steward of mine. Suffering is not a death sentence; it has been an avenue for deeper faith. Life is sticky, joyful and at times really painful; to change one part of my history would change the fabric of me.

Forgiveness:

Finally, genuine forgiveness has thoroughly changed my life from a woman brewing with rage, to a woman of great peace. Forgiveness equals freedom, it does not excuse someone else's behavior, it simply frees me from carrying the weight of someone else's offense. I learned walking in unforgiveness was like drinking poison and expecting other people to die. Most importantly has been the ability to forgive myself and to love the younger me that chose to be voiceless. These concepts were learned and modified from an educational program called Life Skills International.

5 Steps towards Forgiveness:

1. Identify and *feel* the cause of the pain.
2. Choose to forgive; you always have a choice.
3. Identify any self-destructive patterns connected to the event(s).
4. Share your story with a trustworthy person
5. Walk forward in life by focusing on character development and personal growth
   - Use wound specific programs and counseling,
   - Choose to give up self-destructive patterns connected with the event(s). Give yourself grace, this takes practice, sometimes you'll get it right, and

other times you catch yourself running back to old patterns. Dust yourself off and try again,

- Positive words of affirmation (I use the Scriptures)

When I look back at my story, I can say I broke through the numbness, had a season of anger, and now gratefully resting in a place of acceptance. What a miracle! Hope and healing is possible through the Lord Jesus Christ. I am living proof it.

Walking in a new identity:

For decades I wore a costume of a confident woman, but internally I allowed poisonous self-destructive messages to wreak havoc on my mind. They paved the way for how I let others treat me. Allowing my past experiences to determine self-worth was a dangerous and exhausting road. It takes discipline to change the way we think, to arrest a toxic thought and replace it with a positive one. You are worth it! I can joyfully say my identity is no longer derived from my sexuality, or from the acceptance of others, it's not the result of the size of my jeans or the look of my hair. My identity is wholly rooted in how the Lord sees me, nothing else matters! I rest in HIM and so can you.

About Debra Marsalisi

Debra Marsalisi a writer, speaker, and fitness professional. She is on a passionate pursuit of helping others walk in honesty, vulnerability and healing from the past. She began writing to make peace with her life. Writing has provided her with an outlet for creative self-expression, and a healthy new perspective on life which she has the privileged to walk in. Some of her most profound healing moments came from prayer and journaling. Through the grace of God, she has learned to rejoice in life's ups and downs, struggles and victories understanding they been given so she can help and inspire others on their own journey of restoration.

She is an advocate and educator of sexual abuse prevention. As a survivor, thriver, and activist, she is motivated by her desire to support others in emotional and spiritual habits that are truly life-changing. She spends her free time loving, encouraging and mentoring young urban moms; cooking amazing meals for her friends and family.

Check out more of Debra's short stories, poetry and videos at www.DebMarsalisi.com or follow her on Facebook and Instagram @DebMarsalisi

Toxic Cleansing: A Journey of Forgiveness

by Wendy Marquard-Picard

"You have cancer."

Three words can change your life. "I love you", "You are hired", "I am pregnant." Just three words and your world can spin out of control.

"You have cancer" is what the doctor told my mother Alice back in 1997. Stage IV. I stood by the hospital bed unable to move. I brought my mother in because of a persistent cough, never expecting her lifestyle of booze, cigarettes, and marijuana to catch up to her. Mean people don't die. They live on and on to torment those closest to them. Regardless of the years of emotional and physical abuse I had endured, I was heartbroken. This was my mother, and she was going to die very soon.

Then she looked directly at me and said, "This is great! Now I can quit my job and never work again." There was no need for consoling. There were no tears. Just a look of gleeful resignation on her face. The doctor looked confused, but I wasn't. I'd seen that look many times over the years. It was the look she had when she got over on 'the system'. She had succeeded to keep us on welfare until I was ten years old by telling the social worker I was a mentally challenged child that needed her full attention. She had stolen from every job she had. I'd seen the evidence all over the house – a silver platter from an elderly woman she took care of, a gold cross from another, a chipped set of dishes from a large store she was a warehouse packer for. I often wondered why she stole these items. She never used them, never wore them. Maybe it gave her power over something other than me. Maybe, like me, they were her prized possessions. But, like me, she would carelessly handle them. Often, her stolen items would break, but she would keep them anyway.

Alice and her husband Lawrence adopted me when I was a baby. They divorced when I was a toddler, and I never saw my adopted father again. I endured years of resentment and hatred from my adopted mother and never understood why. I spent most of my childhood afraid of what each day would bring. I grew accustomed to being accused of stealing my mother's things she would misplace. I would dodge a slap here and a push there, all the while apologizing for something I didn't do. I learned how to survive in a dangerous world, to be complacent, codependent and no confrontational at a very young age.

Often, Alice would get drunk and rouse me out of bed, no matter the time. I would sit up with her on the opposite couch and listen to her ranting about whatever topic. Many nights very small complaints about me became giant in her mind. She would get so enraged that she would lunge after me, slapping my face or trying to strangle me. I remember thinking one night as she was sitting on top of me with her hands around my neck "She's going to kill me. All because I didn't change the empty toilet paper roll." I would

140

always try to stay one step ahead, checking each night that I cleaned the tables, there was no dirt on the floor, or no dishes in the sink for fear of a beating at two in the morning. Often, I lay in a heap on the floor after one of her belt beatings, punished.

I thought for a very brief moment on that night in the hospital, if anyone <u>deserves</u> cancer, it's HER!

My mother lived for almost two years after her diagnosis. I took care of her until she took her last breath. Those two years were stressful for both of us. When she was diagnosed, I was a newlywed and starting a new career across the country. It was my opportunity to finally get away from the pain and the past. It was my chance to leave my childhood and mother behind – freedom at last! I knew I'd be happy if I could just break away. My husband and I left New England and moved to Arizona to start our new life.

My mother came with us. I couldn't abandon her even though I wanted to. I continued to care for her and carry around my resentment. She was stunting my growth even as an adult. She continued her assault on my psyche daily – angry when I couldn't talk when she called me at work, asking for money to buy needless items, constantly interfering with plans I had with my husband. There were days when I actually felt hatred for this woman. Days when I wondered when she would die so that I could move on with the life I deserved to have. Our relationship was so toxic!

I was alone in the hospital with my mother on the morning she died. I held her hand and told her I loved her. She slipped away. I felt relief, no more suffering for her…or me.

After my mother's death, I settled into my adorable home with my husband and had two beautiful children. I had finally made it, and I was filled with pride. Over the next few years, we would move twice more – once for work and once for the end of our marriage. Never dealing with my codependency before I met my husband led me into another emotionally abusive relationship. I accepted cheating and lies and forgave over and over. Finally, I broke away - again.

After my divorce I knew I <u>wanted</u> happiness, but I honestly didn't know what that meant. I didn't think I'd ever get married again, but God had another plan for me. Hector and I have been blissfully married for nine years now. We have done so much together in these years and have developed a passion for helping those in need. We have such big plans for the future.

"You have cancer."

My life changed earlier this year when my doctor said those three words to <u>me</u>. I could barely hear the rest of the conversation. Breast cancer was someone else's diagnosis, not mine. I got my yearly mammograms and I self-examined monthly. I ate right and exercised. I am a GOOD person! How can I get the same diagnosis that my mother received?

I left the doctor's office and cried in my husband's arms. Why was this happening to *me*?

My oncologists gave me the plan – intense chemotherapy, surgery, radiation and more chemotherapy. I listened to them intently as they explained the side effects of chemo. I felt like I was being punished and I didn't know why.

As I walked into my first round of chemo treatment, I was angry, scared, and confused. I felt fine! I felt completely healthy! I had no symptoms other than a large lump in my breast. Why was I now going to put poison into my system to wreak havoc on my white blood cells? I read every story I could find on the internet, and I talked to everyone I knew that had chemotherapy. All stories were different, and none sounded like fun. I thought of my mother, now dead for almost twenty years. Why is cancer the ONLY thing we have in common? I blamed her for it – not feeding me properly when I was a child, exposing me to second hand cigarette smoke even though I had childhood asthma. I don't remember eating a vegetable that wasn't overcooked in some kind of lard. I was forced to eat pig's feet, fried chicken necks, and other things a farmer would throw away. We were poor and couldn't afford good food, but we *could* afford what I considered my mother's luxuries of alcohol and cigarettes. Why was I still angry about this?

The first day of chemo was a long ten hours. I have a mixture of four different cocktails, plus various meds to keep me from getting nausea or having an allergic reaction. I expected to sleep a lot. Instead I watched patients come and go – all at various ages and different stages in their treatment. I saw a woman that looked very much like Alice. She turned to me and smiled. I didn't smile back because I felt afraid. Of what?

As I sat there receiving bags of medicine, I watched the machine slowly drip the chemicals into my body. I watched for hours before I realized something. It wasn't so much the chemicals being put into my body that day that was toxic. I had been carrying around the toxicity of my relationship with my mother all these years. I never forgave. I continued to carry the hurt and pain inside of me all these years. I knew then I needed to let go to heal my soul before I could heal my body. It is scientific fact that trauma and auto immune diseases are linked. I began to question – why am I here? I finished the first treatment and went home to heal.

The second chemo treatment was twenty-one days later. It takes that long in between for a body to gain back the right amount of strength to be able to handle the next round. At this point I was bald and still angry that I must go through this. I sat down and again watched as the machine dripped its poison into me. I closed my eyes thought of my healing. What did I learn from the first chemo treatment? What will I learn from this one? I prayed for clarity.

I then realized how prideful I had become. Pride is toxic. I convinced myself I had done things differently, way better than my mother did. Pride was a wall I built up to protect myself instead of receiving my true healing. My mother had done the same and had

144

never received peace. I was now forced to look at the ugliness that had built up inside of <u>me</u>. I was hiding behind a façade of blame and shame, carrying my childhood trauma with me, wearing it like armor. It was so heavy, and I wanted it off! I began to cry and asked my mother to forgive me for all the years of blame I placed on her head in order to make me feel like a better person. As I lay there, I started to weave my mother's life and mine together. Perhaps we had more in common than cancer. I knew her childhood was not great either. It doesn't make up for the pain she caused me physically, but she really didn't learn to be a proper parent. I know she was also abused. I remembered my first wedding. She was there even though she was so sick. I asked her to just let me have that one day and not bother me. She couldn't help herself and interrupted my night over and over again. Looking back, what did it matter? I took a breath and let go of the anger. Again, I asked my mother for forgiveness.

My third round of chemo was just this past week. I woke up early, showered, dressed and put on makeup. I walked in with my head held high as I greeted my amazing team of nurses. No fear, no worry. Was I looking forward to chemotherapy? No, but I was determined to use my cancer and its treatment as a catalyst that will also pass and leave me stronger and more resilient to heal emotionally and physically. I was looking forward to what I would learn about myself and what I had the power to change for the better. I prayed for my mother. I prayed for my family and friends that have become my amazing village of love and strength.

As I lay there, drowsy from the medicines, the memory of my mother's funeral came to me. I have to admit that because of the person I imagined her to be, I thought only immediate family would show up. After all, how many friends does a mean person have? I originally picked a small funeral parlor, where we would have a service for her ashes. The next day I changed my mind and selected a larger establishment. I didn't know why I made the change back then, but I know now.

My mother's service was standing room only. Hundreds of people approached me with stories of how she had helped them during a crisis, had sheltered them from an abusive spouse, had given her last dollar because they had none. I was numb that day. There simply could not possibly be so many positive stories about my tyrant of a mother! I listened to them but didn't hear them. For twenty years I still didn't believe that she could be a good person. Now, sitting in my chair, the toxins dripping into me, I remembered every one of the stories, like I was hearing them for the first time. I laughed and I cried. My toxic pride rose again as I thought of the good works my husband and I try to do in the community. I then realized my mother had done so much more to help others than I did. Did she actually teach me to be a good person? I asked again for forgiveness.

Perhaps my mother needed psychiatric help and never received it. There is no excuse when it comes to child abuse. But I'm a survivor and I'm here. I now realize I'm stronger because of her. I know how to raise my children properly because of her. I can tackle cancer because she taught me how to fight for my life. She has become part of the armor I wear into my battle, protecting me now and taking away the damage she had done to me as a child. I imagined putting on my armor and it looks and feels different now. I am a warrior, fighting for my life. I am happy and loved and full of hope.

My fourth chemotherapy will be coming up soon. I try to remain positive every day. The side effects are getting worse with each treatment. I knew it would not be easy. Healing is not easy. However, I am gaining wisdom with each experience. I am being healed emotionally as well. I am learning more about myself each day. I know when to put on my armor and when to be vulnerable without it. I've learned to seek guidance through prayer and therapy that I didn't think I needed in the past. I've learned to forgive and be forgiven. I've let go of anger and have received love.

What will remain is a better me – what will be left is the good my mother sowed into me. And she now has a place in my <u>heart</u> instead of in the tumor.

About Wendy Marquard-Picard

 Wendy Marquard-Picard is a CTA certified life coach, professional organizer and motivational speaker. As the owner of Clutter Coach, LLC d/b/a Clutter Coach Wendy, she is able to create better living and work environments for her clients. She is also the president of Don't Stop Living – a company devoted to inspiring children and adults to achieve the impossible. She and her husband, Hector, are warriors for change and advocates for children with disabilities and other challenges.

A native of Rhode Island, Wendy graduated from Boston College and lived in Massachusetts for many years where she held top positions in the financial publishing field with companies Standard & Poor's and McGraw-Hill. Before starting her own company in 2013, she moved to Arizona and then to the Bahamas to continue her publishing career as a sales director for *Grace Ormonde Wedding Style Magazine.*

Wendy and her golden doodle have contributed over 600 hours of community service to schools, hospitals and nursing homes. She and her husband, two of her four children and various animals live in Fort Lauderdale. She is 'nana' to four grandchildren.

Wendy travels both nationally and internationally where she and her husband speak at schools, corporations, churches and synagogues. Her future goals include traveling to the only U.S. state she has yet to visit (Alaska), jumping out of an airplane, and eventually retiring in Paris.

This is her first published work.

You can connect with Wendy via her websites
www.cluttercoachwendy.com
and
www.dontstopliving.org

CRAWLING OUT OF DARKNESS

By: Terry Gobanga

After dating for a couple of years, Harry proposed to me and I said, "Yes!", I agreed to marry him. I was excited and at the same time overwhelmed, since a lot needed to be done before our that was set for 4th December 2004. This was at the time of my final quarter studying Bible and Theology. Our wedding was scheduled two weeks after my graduation.

Sleep eluded me because of the joy overflowing in my heart. That same night, I realized that I had part of my fiancé's clothes for the wedding. My friend Judy offered to take them to him early next morning. I offered to take her to the bus stop since she wasn't conversant with our neighborhood. I thought, "After all the bus stop was not too far from our house", I convinced myself. I did exactly that and Judy boarded her bus. I started walking back home at a brisk pace as my heart continued to well up with joy, this was my day and I was going to celebrate it. I vaguely noticed a car parked right in front of me after walking through a short alley. There was a man seated on the hood of the car whilst talking on his phone and another on the other side of the car. I did not give them any thought.

I got to the car and as I made my way to pass it, the man sitting on the hood grabbed me from behind and his hand covered my mouth. I was about to scream but the guy was swift enough to ensure that the sound was muffled. I was shoved in the car with the guy who was outside, helping to push my tall frame inside the car, as I kicked out in frantic effort to fight them off. We drove off immediately and to my horror I realized there was a third man who was the driver. For a split second I thought this was not real, perhaps Harry was trying to surprise me, but these thoughts quickly vanished when one of them hit me ordered me to cooperate or else I would die.

By this time my mouth had been stuffed with something which I later realized were pieces of cloth. The guy who was in the back seat with me, started reaching out for my denim pants in a rough way. He kept shouting at me and continued hitting me, while the guy was in the driver's seat just kept threatening me with the knife, he held in his hands swinging it carelessly back and forth. I struggled against their vile intentions, but I was overpowered, and the worst happened; I was raped while in that moving car. It was painful and filthy. As I was battling with many thoughts in my mind including how I could just get to the knife and stab one or all of them, the second guy came to the back seat and he too raped me. The car stopped briefly and now it was the drivers turn. One of my assailants took over the driving and the car was on the move again. This man, he removed the pieces of clothe from my mouth, opened up his zipper with a leg across my face. While clutching my mouth he warned me not to do anything stupid or I he would kill me. He proceeded to put his manhood in my mouth. By this time, I figured that these brutes would kill me anyway and I knew I had nothing more to lose, so I summoned all my guts and bit him hard, so that he would never do this to another lady again. He groaned in pain and hit me hard on my face, the car door was opened, and I was thrown out after being stabbed in the stomach. I remember hitting the ground hard and I passed out. I later learnt of how I was rescued and taken to hospital and it was indeed a miracle.

I got treated at the hospital, but then recovery was not an easy process. I was in a whirlpool of rage and confusion. I wondered how I did not think there was danger ahead. I was angry at God for not protecting me. My mind and my heart were bogged down in a flood of emotions. I had more questions than answers. Family and friends got to learn that I had been found and I was alive. They had been searching for me from the time I disappeared. The wedding plans had been put on hold because I was at large.

One media outlet got wind of the story and my story was aired on prime-time news. I was angry and felt naked and ashamed.

I was put on ARVS as a precautionary measure to protect me against the HIV virus and also given medication to help prevent conception. I was stitched in my tummy wound and the doctor told me I would not conceive since the stab wound had raptured by womb in a terrible way. I was devastated but thankfully Harry was by my side through it all. In fact, he wanted me to marry him in hospital so that we could go home for him to take care of me. My thoughts were all jumbled up and I wasn't in the right frame of mind.

I went through counseling and after about 6 months, I was to walk down the aisle. Harry was so delighted, and we started planning our 'second wedding' since the first one did not work out. We had no money given the first one had depleted our finances. A total stranger by the name Vip reached out to me with an unbelievable idea. She told me, "Together with a group of 3 other ladies we will give you a free wedding". I was elated, ecstatic and besides myself. God had come through for me. The wedding arrangements started, and my fiancé hired a bodyguard to be by my side. He didn't want to take any chances and more so, because the police had not come up with any leads about my perpetrators.

We had a beautiful, grand big wedding. Many people came and witnessed God's faithfulness; the police were also there just to ensure that the event runs smoothly. God provided for us through his child, VIP.

We went for our honeymoon which was fully paid for us as well and had a wonderful time amidst challenges since I was only 7 months shy from the rape ordeal. After 3 weeks of reconnecting, resting, relaxing and reigniting our dreams, we came back to Nairobi where we had signed a lease into a new house. We were a new couple, ready to take on the world with new possibilities. On Saturday morning we agreed to fast and pray as we started our married life. As the day progressed, I told my husband I wanted to go to the saloon and do my hair. He agreed to accompany me. After we got there, he decided that he wanted to buy a charcoal burner that he would use to warm the house. I was a bit reluctant because the burner fumes normally affect my breathing. After haggling back and forth, I grudgingly accepted.

He explained to me that he would light it up then take it to the bedroom for some time and then take it out as we went to bed. He did exactly that and for sure the room was warm and nice. As I was cooking in the kitchen he came and switched of the gas saying we need to talk. I wondered what was so urgent that we had to talk at that moment. He told me in case he dies, then I should go on with my life and get married. I had come from a close-knit family; I would need someone…I continued listening to him, but I didn't want to hear that kind of talk. We were a young couple that had just come back from our honeymoon, spent the whole day in prayer and fasting and now preparing to eat, sleep and wake up head to church. I was a Pastor who was looking forward to being by my husband's side. He was not happy that I stopped him, but we embraced after a while, cried and prayed.

After our meal we went to the bedroom and it was warm and nice, but I was still feeling cold. Harry asked me to wear a hoodie, he went on to lock up the doors and when he came back, he said he was feeling dizzy. We did not make anything much of it but from the time we got to bed we were so cold and after a while we were not able to even stand due to lack of strength. We kept passing out and regaining consciousness. I managed to call my maid of honor who was our neighbor, she came to our aid and rushed us to hospital.

At the hospital, when I regained consciousness, I asked where my husband was, and I was told he was in the next emergency room and the doctors were working on him. For some reason, I had a gut feeling that all was not well with Harry, the medical personnel could not allow me to leave my room.

After a while I overheard a nurse having a conversation with someone on the phone and the words that caught my attention were, ".... Do not close the morgue, we have a client". I froze as the hair on my nape stood up. I just needed to ensure that client was not my Harry. After calling for the doctor frantically to tell me where my husband was, my fears were confirmed, Harry was dead, my husband of 29 days was dead! This blow just shattered me to pieces.

Back at my parents' house again and I started the arduous task of planning my late husband's funeral. Many busybodies were propelling rumors about my involvement in Harry's death. I asked for a post mortem, and thank God for a supportive role that family took to ensure this was done. The results showed his cause of death was carbon monoxide poisoning. I somehow survived because at that moment when we were slipping in and out of consciousness, I threw up and this had allowed me to release some of the poison. The pathologist also said Harry had chocked from the food we had just eaten, since food was found on his trachea. Sadness and numbness crowned my days, because I could not just make sense of all that had happened.

After a few years of making it very public that I would never get married again, since God took away my husband, I got married to a wonderful, loving man, I call him my package wrapped by God himself and delivered to me. His name is Tony and he has continued to be very supportive in every season. I was harboring a cocktail of emotions that I had carried from my trying seasons and there were times when I would be okay and there are times when the emotions would explode in waves. What amazes me is his commitment and consistency to love. On our fourth day of meeting me, he told me that he would marry me. God had opened a new chapter in my story. I was okay with the fact that I might never conceive as that is what the doctor had told me, but after one year of marriage we were blessed with a baby girl. Today we are blessed with two most adorable daughters. It was not an easy ride especially the first one as I was on bed rest, but His faithfulness is unmatched.

God started impressing upon me to share my story and He gave me the grace and boldness to do it. It wasn't easy to come out and talk about the dark shadows of my life. When I started sharing and I felt naked but with time, God's grace has grown in me and I see myself as a weapon in His hands ready to be released whenever and wherever. Since then I haven't looked back, as the Lord continues to open so many doors in my country and abroad, I get to speak in conferences and corporations, while wearing different hats as He would need me to depend on the door opened. As a motivational speaker I find it fulfilling when I see people's faces light up knowing it's not how deep in the gutter one is but the little steps you make to get out and that people can only go so far in helping you, the rest of the work is dependent on an individual's drive to see themselves better. Together with my husband we are the visionaries of Stones to Rubies Ministries a growing, vibrant church.

My book "Crawling out of Darkness" was birthed in 2011 amidst tears as I had to peel back the memories in order for me to be able to bring forth every word without wearing a mask as it is with many people and yet inside, they are dying. I wanted to be real and show that even born-again believers suffer and end up questioning God at times, but His mercy and saving grace brings us back to Him.

Awards have been given to me for the work I do amongst the women and children in my country to empower them and rescue the children that need to be rescued from sexual assault. My greatest joy is when I am able to speak life to a parent who is giving up because of the rape ordeal the child has gone through and feels it's the end but I come in to assure them, it is not over and that given a chance their daughter can be whole again if we work as a team. After years of counselling trauma victims, I felt that it was not enough since some had to go back to the same environment and especially the rape survivors. So, I decided to start a half-way house where girls aged 14 years old and below are brought to us and we stay with them for a period of one year as we give them therapy of different kinds, while allowing them to keep going on with their "normal" life e.g. school. Once we see a child is ready, we reintegrate them back to the society not as a survivor but as a warrior ready to conquer their fear. You can find out more about us here www.karaolmurani.org and support us as you can.

"Dare to dream again" is what I keep telling people around me. It's not in the big steps, it's in the crawling you start today because when life beats you down so hard, it takes so much strength to stand back up and walk but crawling is still some movement because destiny awaits.

About Terry Gobanga

 Terry Gobanga is a minister who hails from Kenya. She is married to Rev. Tonny Gobanga and they are blessed with two daughters, Tehille and Towdah. They are the visionaries of Stones to Rubies Ministries International founded in 2012. She is an alumnus of East Africa University where she graduated in Bible and Theology.

She is also the President and founder of Kara Olmurani, a community-based organization in Kenya that serves as a safe haven for young girls who have been sexually assaulted.

www.karaolmurani.org

In 2016, she was awarded The Timeless Woman of Wonder Award, for her community work among women and in 2017 she was honored to receive the Café Ngoma Humanitarian Award for the work she does amongst rape survivors.

She has been featured by many media platforms including the BBC. Today, she speaks with an endearing charisma in conferences and corporate organizations all over the globe with a message of hope and encouragement.

Terry's autobiography, crawling out of Darkness, captures her life's journey from the dungeons of despair to a life full of promise.

www.terrygobanga.com   terrygobanga@gmail.com

Living from Worthy

By: Dr. Andrea Hazim

"If you don't know WHO you are and WHY you are here, life can be a twisted maze of disappointments, experienced like you are trying to navigate through a thick overgrown forest in the dark, blindfolded, handcuffed, and wearing ear plugs. It isn't pretty."

In a short time, I'm going to take you on a journey that brought me from uncertainty, to an absolute knowing of my true identity and purpose. And then I'm going to show how you can do it too! Let's jump right in.

Wise in My Own Eyes

Finalizing his police report, the officer stopped writing and asked, "Do you want to press charges?" As his question hung in the air, I stood frozen, studying the stranger I called "my husband." It was fascinating that this person, filled with enough rage to strike me to the ground one minute, could seem so cool and collected the next. Dressed in a freshly pressed shirt and tie, he appeared to be a smug businessman. His mocking smirk so threatening, it prompted a quick, "No." It was my only safe reply. No sooner had the officer walked out, then loneliness, doubt, and regret rushed in. I ignored the urge to yell, "Wait, and arrest him before he hurts me again!"

Fear and shame hid my life in a domestic violence prison. The abusive warden was free to wreak emotional and physical havoc. Within the first thirty days of marriage, vows of love were tainted by shock and betrayal, emotional adultery, episodes of rage, and even a threat of murder. He was skilled at physical abuse without leaving a mark, but the emotional wounds inflicted were devastating. My heart was crushed when he casually dismissed my dreams; "I already have two children, so I won't be reversing my vasectomy."

How foolish I had been to disregard the advice of friends and family when they attempted to point out multiple red flags. A pastor warned, "If you were my daughter, I would tell you to run!" Friends voiced their grave concern about my once lively demeanor, now withdrawn, wilted like a listless faded flower. A trampled garden perfectly depicted the abusive life I was living, estranged from friends, family, and God.

The day the police were summoned to my apartment was also the day my rescuer appeared. In the clinic that afternoon, a long-standing patient immediately sensed my distress and insisted I tell her what was wrong. Her love and concern broke through my defenses. The hidden truth came out and without discussion, she led me like a lost child to the safety of her home. You can imagine the relief that washed over me when I entered her beautiful guest room. The picture-perfect bedding became a cocoon of refuge. My body surrendered to months of weariness and emotional exhaustion.

The stage was set for an epic paradigm shift. Like it or not, my understanding of "SELF" and identity would soon be supernaturally realigned forever. When I awoke, instead of desiring water, it was an unquenchable and urgent thirst for clarity that I sensed. The desperate need for revelation and restoration superseded all else. I resolved to eat nothing until I got answers. There was a ticker-tape of investigative questions clicking through my brain. Broken and humbled, I needed to understand... "What is my problem? How did I get here? Why hadn't I heeded advice? Who am I? What do I do now?"

SELF-sabotaging M.O.

Three tear-filled days of seclusion and contemplation passed when my closest friend suddenly appeared at the door. She insisted that I go with her to a women's conference. Thirty minutes later, I miraculously found myself amidst thousands of women in a supercharged arena. Alone in a crowd, I sat tortured by the four-word mantra, "What is my problem?" I could focus on little else and the growing frustration wore on me.

I was getting nothing out of this and was just about to exit, when the divine intervened. A curious vision caught my eye. It looked like an illuminated Broadway sign flashing above the speaker's head. Just one word— REBELLION. I plopped back down, mesmerized by this heavenly billboard. Was it meant just for me? Was this God's answer? He had my full attention. Nine letters, R-E-B-E-L-L-I-O-N.

Then internal alarms sounded, "whoop-whoop-whoop," from the recesses of my soul. High-speed divine downloads of four familiar words came to the forefront of my mind: INDEPENDENT

- COMPETENT - ACHIEVER - SURVIVOR, missing pieces to my inner puzzle. But, how did they fit together? God knew I had minimal experience with SELF-inquiry and even less training in how to grow or heal emotionally. I loved that He encountered me in a visual way. My soul and spirit were taking it all in, but my hand could barely keep up as I journaled about each word...

Rebellion - *opposition to one in authority ; defiance, resistance*

Independent - *Self-governing; not requiring or relying on someone or something else; not subject to control by others*

Competent - *having the capacity to function or develop; qualified, adequate*

Achiever - *to get or attain as the result of exertion; accomplish*

Survivor - *to remain alive or in existence; to live on*

These words hallmarked the way I did life and is why I was handicapped to take advice from authorities, including God. But suddenly a scripture resounded in my heart. *"God will open the eyes of the blind and unplug the ears of the deaf."* I prayed this would become true in my life. It is sobering to realize that blind and deaf ignorance leads to such consequences.

Overlapping word pictures emerged as pieces came into place. I saw how the parallel tracks, REBELLION and INDEPENDENT, were derailing my life. The pièce de résistance was when I discovered God's heart on rebellion; *"Rebellion is as the sin of witchcraft, and stubbornness is as idolatry."*

Diving deeper, I began to understand the state of my mental operating system:

Rebellion - *opposition to one in authority; defiance, resistance.*

At six years old, my parents divorced, and I emotionally divorced them! In the ugly aftermath I lost respect for authorities. Raised by a mom who mistrusted everyone, and whom could be told what to do by no one, especially men, it became a breeding ground for rebellion.

Sin - *a vitiated state in which SELF is estranged from God.*

My lone-ranger SELF had made enough detrimental choices apart from God. I was ready to begin the great adventure. God promises, "more than we could ask, think or imagine" IF we exercise the faith to choose His plan for our lives.

Witchcraft - *an irresistible influence or fascination; use of sorcery or magical powers.*

It was revolting, but accurate, to see myself as a witch. I had worked MY magic for MY desired outcomes, stubbornly forging ahead with MY will. It came at too great a price that I was no longer willing to pay!

Stubbornness - *refusing to change your ideas or to stop doing something; difficult to deal with.*

Headstrong, self-willed, and unrelenting were strong synonyms that pointed back to my inability to heed good advice or respect authority.

164

Idolatry - *to worship as a god; immoderate attachment or devotion to something*

A misplaced devotion to calling the shots and an attachment to stubbornness prevented any consideration of God's plan for my life. The time had come to stop worshiping at the altar of "Me, Myself, and I."

These puzzle pieces started resembling a double helix sequence of words, which had negatively programed my mental and emotional DNA.

Living from WORTHY

Let's admit that teenagers are not alone in acting like they know it all. We are all vulnerable to the blindness that prevents us from recognizing we are "Wise in our own eyes" and "We don't know what we don't know." Self-destructive behaviors like pride, bitterness, unforgiveness, shame, fear, and others, become obstacles to our greatness. I call these the "Slimes of SELF-sabotage." And I was plagued with them. Living with them is like committing spiritual suicide. Enough was enough; I was ready to fully embrace my true IDENTITY.

Identity - *the fact of being who or what a person or thing is.*

This is so vague. Finding the answer to "WHO you are" is precisely the point. No wonder there is an identity crisis plaguing our world!

As I explored IDENTITY in scripture, the encounter between God and my SELF continued. Each journal entry miraculously filled the cracked and empty places inside of me...

- I am God's child, whom He lovingly created with a unique plan and purpose.
- I am united with God and receive His Spirit through the sacrifice of His Son Jesus.
- I am confident that the healing work God has begun in me will be completed, producing abundant fruit in my life.
- I am a worthy Daughter of the King, a royal heir and citizen of heaven.

This was a turbo boost to my low Self-worth, which had been one of those subconscious slimes, causing so many setbacks in my life. One such, falling prey to marrying an abusive man. I had slimed myself by believing I was damaged goods, unworthy and disqualified from having a healthy marriage.

What happened next is the fairytale I previously considered myself unworthy of. Space does not permit the details, but I will sum it up like this. The abusive marriage ended when my husband refused to reform. With that chapter closed, and armed with a new identity and spiritual rebirth, one no longer rooted in self-sabotage, but instead self-worth, I was ready to embrace all that God had for me. He first revealed a list of qualities of the man I would marry. Then, three months later on a mission trip, He gave me that man.

And as I write, we just celebrated 20 glorious years together, including the gift of three amazing sons.

A New Outlook

Over those years, I've gained new tools to improve my life. In my early forties, I followed a trusted friend's advice and participated in a Personal Mastery weekend. At one point, the facilitator said, "Share something that impacted your life." I offered the devastating saga of my parents' spiteful divorce. I included the accompanying tales of heartbreak from my Dad, who I considered my ballroom dancing Prince Charming when I was a little girl. He remarried and divorced three successive stepmothers. I added the details about the emotionally unhealthy life I was forced to live with my mom.

The facilitator then asked, "What did that mean?" I wasn't conscious that it "meant" anything, but my account revealed buried shame, resentment, anger, and unforgiveness. A sense of potential breakthrough urged me to dig deeper. I was shocked by my reply, "It means...what nice stable guy would want to marry me, a girl from a crazy broken family?" Instant clarity! My subconscious belief of being "UNWORTHY" had set low standards, causing me to settle for Mr. Wrong.

The facilitator's demeanor invited me to go deeper; "What does it REALLY mean?" You could sense the mental gears turning in the room. Then, click, the REAL meaning came. It was simple; my dad remarried multiple times, and my mother was emotionally unstable.

That's it. What? My emotionally embellished story about my parents had led to years of mistaken identity and distorted self-worth. In one paradigm-shifting moment I was set free from the false belief that my father's failed marriages and mother's emotions meant anything about my worthiness. I had just personally experienced the power in the scripture; "Be transformed by the renewing of your mind."

Discovering identity and purpose is paramount to a fulfilling and abundant life! It frustrates me to see rates of self-harm and suicide increase each year. Sadly, training in transformational life skills is hard to come by, especially during impressionable teen years when it could make the biggest impact. I am so grateful for the knowledge and skills I have gained in my adult years and teaching these skills to future generations is of utmost importance. If they gain these tools early in life, they can avoid wasting years being emotionally unequipped, creating false "meanings," and perpetuating stinkin-thinkin. Had I gained these practical life skills in my teen years, without a doubt, I would have known how to: reject unworthiness, deal with personality conflicts, communicate effectively, forgive quickly, and avoid resentment.

Resilience Conditioning

I have a deep appreciation for growing up in a hard-working family where my parents, aunts, uncles and grandparents modeled a relentless work ethic. I have many fond memories of participating in elaborate Sunday Italian dinners. I was enrolled in every aspect of the meal: cooking, setting the table, cleaning the kitchen, and even gardening.

At six years old my parents' divorce began and my healthy childhood ended. Being the firstborn, I was enrolled as my single mom's right hand, which had various pros and cons. I enjoyed tackling the hard things required, but her standards of perfection made pleasing her impossible. It wasn't until I took myself to a counselor in my early twenties that I discovered that the unhealthy environment during my adolescent development created emotional enmeshment with my mother.

Mom's unspoken rule: **IF** you like what she liked and hate who she hated (namely my dad), a peaceful day may be achieved. Rather than being overtly rebellious, I learned to adapt to the murky water that I had to swim in. Thus, the seeds of INDEPENDENT - COMPETENT - ACHIEVER - SURVIVOR were planted. Many days it looked like taking two Tylenol on the way home from school to divert an inevitable stress headache. Daydreams became a mental refuge where I would imagine, "One day I will..." leave home, be my own person, have a voice, and create a life on my terms. Until then, *smile and wave.*

I've learned that any strength, when overextended, becomes a weakness that easily hurts the ones closest to us. Regardless of emotional struggles with my parents, I acknowledge that some of those struggles are actually the flip-side of their hard work and resilience. They modeled doing hard things, self-confidence, courage and boldness. It has become my tradition to teach young leaders that "Hard is the New Fun!"

Be encouraged that no matter how messy life gets, or how devastating the setbacks, your experiences develop an UNSTOPPABLE resilience that no life is without! I love that God is in the business of "turning our mess into our message." As a young adult, I was completely ill-equipped to handle life's setbacks or the emotional challenges that go along with them. Today my heart leaps every time I have the privilege of helping a teen or college-age student identify where they are stuck. There is nothing like seeing young leaders' breakthrough the Slimes of SELF-sabotage, live with purpose, develop RESILIENCE, and achieve SUCCESS in life.

Resilience - the power or ability to recover; elasticity; buoyancy.

Success - *favorable or desired outcome*

Vision for Tomorrow's Leaders Today

The quality of our mental, emotional, and even spiritual life is roughly:

- 10% what actually happens
- 90% what we decide it will "mean" and how that "meaning" affects our identity and future choices

Healthy interpretations lead to mature responses. The ability to respond rather than react is a life skill, which must be consciously learned and consistently practiced. A perfect illustration of mature behavior is the Fruit of the Spirit: love, joy, peace, patience, kindness, goodness, faithfulness, gentleness, and self-control.

Have you noticed an epidemic of unconscious purposeless living? A lack of identity breeds instability. Young and old, and those of every race and gender, add to the devastating statistics each year. Increasingly, lives are destroyed through self-harm and suicide; addictive behaviors such as pornography, social media, alcohol, and drug use; and other "slimes"!

Think of the teens and college-age young adults in your life, then catch the vision to see future generations who know their identity and live with purpose, at a young age! My life is dedicated to fulfilling that vision. I often tell young adults they are Pure Potential! It is awe inspiring to see young leaders fully engaged during an experiential leadership program like iDENTIFY IMPACT's week-long intensive. There is nothing more rewarding than watching them discover their self-worth, identity, and purpose, while being equipped with critical life skills in communication, team building, conflict resolution, recognizing personality types, and developing empathy.

Its time! It's time to shift culture; time to harness pure potential; and definitely time to raise up "TLT," (Tomorrow's Leaders Today)

About Andrea Hazim

 Dr. Andrea has a clear vision to cultivate future generations of "TLT," Tomorrow's Leaders Today. For over two decades, she has been empowering clients and audiences as an educator, author, and speaker.

Her purpose to "Impact Lives" launched at nineteen in London, England while completing an International Massage Certification. Furthering her education, she earned two bachelor's Degrees (Nutrition and Dietetics) and Doctor of Chiropractic.

During a medical mission in Panama, Central America, divine appointment led Andrea to meet Dr. Jeff Hazim. Their "Hazim Team" soon grew to include three sons and added parenting, home education, curriculum development and youth leadership to Andrea's skill set.

She has produced many educational events and co-authored the "Lessons for Healthy Living" series. After selling a thriving practice, Full Stature Consulting became a portal for individuals and organizations to get laser-focused on WHO they are, WHERE they are going, and HOW they will get there.

Dr. Andrea Hazim is considered an expert in training teen students and college-age mentors to discover their identity and walk in their purpose. Her vast experience in education and leadership development revealed an urgent need to equip young adults with critical life-skills. As Founder and President of the Elev8Life educational foundation, she developed three transformational serving leadership programs:

- **IDENTIFY IMPACT** 7-day/6-night experiential summer intensive
- **TLT Travel Ambassadors** opportunity to stand, lead and serve
- **"Wisdom Keepers' Series"** literary project honoring senior generations' wisdom in the book series "Grey is the Original Google"

Learn more about unique training opportunities for young adults to rise above average as Tomorrow's Leaders Today...

Connect with Andrea online at www.Dr.AndreaHazim.com or email at DrAnj@Elev8Life.org

Visit **iDENTIFYimpact.com** to learn more about transformational opportunities for young adults to rise above average and become Tomorrow's Leaders Today.

PART III

The Power of Intentionality:

Cultivate Non-Judgment

Climb Your Mountain

Face Your Fears to Achieve New Heights

By: Ginger Martin

In February 2015, I took time off work as CEO of a bank in Florida and traveled 8,000 miles to Africa to do the hardest thing I had ever done in my life. At the age of 57, I was there with The Freedom Challenge to climb Mt Kilimanjaro, the highest free-standing mountain in the world at 19,341 ft. As I gazed across the plains of Tanzania, the massive bulk of Kilimanjaro loomed, dwarfing everything in the surrounding area, and I felt small. I suddenly questioned my decision to take on this challenge. Drawing a deep breath, I reminded myself why I was there: to fight the social injustice of global and domestic human trafficking, a cause which I am deeply passionate about.

Before I tell you the story and the lessons I learned from the journey, I want to pause and ask you something.

Are there days when you feel like you are climbing a mountain?

Does your job, career, or business feel overwhelming – like you are going uphill?

Do you struggle with doubts, fears, insecurities and uncertainties?

Do you worry about making the right decisions or missing an opportunity?

Do you ever ask yourself if you are good enough – if you have what it takes?

Do you have times when things seem too hard and you want to quit?

Does handling the multiple responsibilities of career, family, finances, health and relationships seem exhausting – maybe like climbing a mountain?

I am convinced, more than ever, that mountains are symbolic of life. Life is an uphill journey. Anything worth having requires effort, and we cannot coast to success.

So, let me take you on my 7-day, 6-night journey of climbing Kilimanjaro with 19 other climbers.

Kilimanjaro is an extinct volcano. The rim is covered with glaciers and ice fields. I couldn't believe that in a few hours, I would begin my climb of this HUGE Mountain. I was suddenly overwhelmed by feelings of fear and doubt!

Day 1: We started our journey at the elevation of 6,400 ft. The first day was relatively easy. We went through forests and fields and even though we gained 2,200 ft. of elevation, it was not that hard. We had 100 porters and guides carrying everything we would need for the 7 days and 6 nights on the mountain. Our first camp was at 8,600 ft. There were still grass and trees at this elevation, and the temperature was mild.

Day 2: We gained 2,900 ft. of elevation. As we made our way up the mountain, we heard a constant Swahili phrase from our guides – POLE, POLE (po-lay). It means slowly, slowly. It became our mantra! The guides kept us at a slow and steady pace, so our bodies could adjust to the increasing altitude. The other phrase we heard was SIPPY, SIPPY. It was critical we drank lots of water because staying hydrated also prevents altitude sickness, a potentially life-threatening condition. People die on Kilimanjaro every year.

We camped the second night at 11,500 ft., and this was where our first climber succumbed to altitude sickness. As I watched her hunched over with nausea, I wondered if this could happen to me. I laid in my tent worrying about what the next day would hold. How hard would it be? Would I be able to keep up? What if I got altitude sickness and had to be taken off the mountain? To deal with my fears, I prayed and said a verse repeatedly "For God hath not given us (me) the spirit of fear; but of power, and of love, and of a sound mind" 2 Timothy 1:7 KJV.

Day 3: Our third camp was at 13,000 ft. This would be our acclimatization camp, and we spent 2 nights here. When we first got to camp, we had lunch, rested for a few hours, and then hiked up 45 minutes higher than the camp, before coming back down to spend the night. There is no vegetation at this level, only dirt and rocks, and the temperatures are much colder. Our second climber fell ill at this altitude. The following morning, he was put on an IV because of the dehydration from vomiting and diarrhea.

Day 4: We went higher than the day before to 14,725 ft. and came back to 13,000 ft. This process again gave our bodies the chance to acclimate to the challenge of the increasing altitude. When we got to camp later that afternoon, we learned that the ill climber had been evacuated by the porters. The evacuation further heightened my own doubts, fears and apprehensions of what the next day would hold.

Day 5: We moved to Kibo Camp at 15,500 ft. It was from here we would make our summit attempt. When we got to this camp, we had lunch and were told to get our gear ready. I tried to sleep even though it was the middle of the afternoon because we would be getting up at 10 p.m. to eat and begin the summit attempt. At this altitude, where the oxygen level is reduced, it is an effort to do even the simplest things, like tie your shoes. By this time, we had been on the mountain 5 days, sleeping in tents with no showers or other comforts. The wind was gusting so hard, my tent was shaking, and the noise was deafening. I put my ear plugs in and tried to go to sleep. My anxiety level was at an all-time high.

I started asking myself questions:

Do I have what it takes?

Am I strong and fit enough?

What if I don't make it to the summit?

What if I get altitude sickness?

Again, I am praying and reciting 2 Timothy 1:7.

We left at 11:30 p.m. that night. It was cold, dark and frightening. The uncertainty of what lay ahead pushed me way out of my comfort zone. The fear of the unknown was overwhelming.

We had on head lamps and multiple layers of clothes, and each of us was assigned a guide for the summit attempt. We started out as a group, but within the first few hours our group drifted apart in the dark as climbers moved at varying paces, and I found myself alone with my guide, Tito, walking ahead of me. I remember wishing Tito was behind me because the trail was so steep, I had the sensation of falling backwards. The higher we went, the harder it was to breathe.

All I could do was look at my boots and Tito's boots in front of me. I didn't know if I could keep going. He kept repeating "we are moving". I think he felt he needed to remind me of this because I was barely moving, struggling against the cold and the blackness to just put one foot in front of the other.

At this point, it became a mental feat for me because my body was at its physical limits, I was exhausted, my legs ached, I could hardly breathe, and I was light headed. The water in the reservoir of my Camel Back had frozen, and ice was floating in my water bottle. I started telling myself to take one more step, and then one more step – because each step represents one more woman, one more child, one more life that could be rescued from human trafficking. At one point, I asked Tito if we were on the trail because we were using our hands to climb over boulders, and I could not even see where we were going. When I look back on that night, I am so thankful for Tito because he had done this climb many times before and knew the way, even in the dark with no trail.

Day 6: At 5:30 a.m., after gaining 3,100 ft. elevation and 6 hours of steep, hard climbing, we reached the rim of Kilimanjaro at Gilman's Point, 18,600 ft. We were greeted with a glorious sunrise. We were not at the summit yet, but at least it was not dark and not as steep. However, we still had a long way to go.

Two hours later, at 7:30 a.m., 8 hours after I started, I stood on the summit of Kilimanjaro at Uhuru Peak, 19,341 ft.!!! The view was amazing, and I was exhilarated despite my exhaustion.

I was celebrating and taking pictures, when the realization hit me: I am only half way! I must get back down! I'll give you the short version. It took me 4 hours to get back to Kibo Hut. When I first entered the mess tent, I was shaking so badly I could not even hold a cup. Someone had to help me drink and eat like a child. I realized I had not eaten and drunk enough on the way down, probably because I was not thinking clearly due to the altitude, and I was depleted of energy. I found one of my fellow climbers in the mess tent on oxygen because her altitude sickness was so severe. She had summited though! She ended up being taken down by porters to the next camp in a metal cart that resembled a wheel barrel. I also learned another climber had turned back after 3 hours of climbing on the summit attempt. After eating, drinking and resting, I started feeling better and began the final stage of the day from 15,500 ft. to the Horombo camp at 12,000 ft. It was the longest 6 miles of my life. I felt like the Israelites, wandering in the wilderness for 40 years. I didn't think I would ever reach my destination.

After 16 hours of hiking that day, I laid in my tent that night, physically, mentally, and emotionally exhausted. All I could think about was whether I would be able to walk the 12 miles and descend the 6,000 ft. that would be required the next day. I was worried. Thankfully, I had a good night's sleep and woke up feeling better than I expected.

Day 7: As we set out on the final 12 miles of our journey, I had a lot of time to reflect on the experience. For the past 6 days, I had just been trying to survive, but I realized there were many similarities between life and climbing mountains: the ups and downs, the peaks and valleys and plateaus, the mental toughness it requires.

I did make those 12 miles and was welcomed by a group of porters and guides singing and celebrating our success. When I looked around 2 climbers were not there. They were not able to complete the 12 miles and were brought down by porters.

I had respect for the 2 climbers who did not summit. Some might say they failed in their mission. However, while they did not make it to the top of Kilimanjaro, they had the courage and conviction to get out of their comfort zones and do something to help others. Thanks to the efforts of a team of 20 everyday, ordinary people, this climb raised $800,000 to fight human trafficking!

You may not ever find yourself on Kilimanjaro, but we are all climbing symbolic mountains. Consider for a moment - what is your next mountain, your next goal, your next dream? You will find there is always another mountain to climb. Just like life, climbing a mountain is hard, it is risky, it takes preparation and training, the weather is unpredictable, sometimes cold, dark, windy and rainy. It is dangerous and uncertain. It has its overwhelming challenges and its spectacular peaks.

I want to leave you with some of the lessons I learned from Kilimanjaro to inspire and encourage you on your own journey.

HAVE A COMPELLING WHY. A passion to live for something that is bigger than you. A dream. If I had attempted to climb Kilimanjaro without having the "WHY" of fighting human trafficking, I likely would have quit when it got hard on summit night.

BE PREPARED. Climbing mountains takes hard work, training and preparation, just like life. You don't just wake up one day and decide to climb Kilimanjaro and succeed. Have grit and determination. Put thought into what you want to achieve and keep showing up.

POLE, POLE. Go at your own pace. Be patient. Allow yourself the time to enjoy the journey. Stop to catch your breath so you don't burn yourself out on the way. You don't go from the bottom of Kilimanjaro to the summit without making stops along the way.

DON'T COMPARE. It is so easy to compare ourselves to others. We often think someone else is more talented or better or further up the mountain than we are. Comparison is the thief of happiness. Just be the best version of you. On Kilimanjaro, it didn't matter who got to the summit first or last or even if we didn't reach it. Even titles, position and status don't matter on the mountain.

ACCLIMATIZATION. Acclimatization is defined by Merriam-Webster as adopting to a new temperature, altitude, climate, environment, or situation. Sounds like business and life, doesn't it? We are always adjusting and adapting to different challenges and situations just like we did on Kilimanjaro. Remember the 2 nights we spent at 13,000 ft.? We went up and came back down. The next day we went higher than the day before and came back down. It is the same with life. If you think you are making progress but find yourself where you started, don't get discouraged. Don't think you have failed or lost ground. Sometimes we must come back down to be able to go higher than we have ever gone before.

TAKE ONE MORE STEP – KEEP MOVING.

Finally, when you feel you can't go on, when you've reached your limit and you want to give up, take one more step and then one more step. Keep moving in the direction of your goal or dream. Consistency and discipline are keys to success. We are all capable of doing so much more than we think we can.

You have come this far in your journey, keep going, keep climbing. When you are standing on top of the mountain, the struggles and challenges, the doubts and fears, fade from your memory because the views are breathtaking, and the sense of accomplishment is overwhelming.

Go climb your mountain! Be Unstoppable!

"I lift my eyes to the mountains – where does my help come from? My help comes from the Lord, the Maker of heaven and earth." Psalm 121:1 NIV.

**** To learn more about The Freedom Challenge and the many ways to get involved, please go to:
https://www.thefreedomchallenge.com/ ****

About Ginger Martin

President and Chief Executive Office, American National Bank

As President and CEO of American National Bank, Ms. Martin is not only known to run a successful community bank, but as a fervent community leader, anti-human trafficking activist and an advocate for women's professional development and growth.

Ms. Martin's passion for fighting against human trafficking has led her on a mountain climbing journey with The Freedom Challenge since 2014. With six climbs under her belt thus far, including a noteworthy climb of Mt. Kilimanjaro in 2015, Machu Picchu in 2017, and Mt. Whitney in 2018, Ms. Martin has tirelessly raised funds and awareness for the cause. As a result, Ms. Martin has been asked to speak to a multitude of different groups throughout South Florida, including a 2018 TEDx Talk.

Under her leadership, the bank has received numerous awards for its financial performance and community involvement, such as the *Banky Award* from The Institute for Extraordinary Banking for the last 3 years, *Business of the Year Award* from South Florida Business Journal, and *Small Business of the Year* from the Greater Fort Lauderdale Chamber of Commerce. The Commonwealth Institute named the bank one of the "Top 50 Women Led Businesses" in the state of Florida for 5 consecutive years.

In addition, Ms. Martin has been personally honored for her business leadership with awards such as *Ultimate CEO* by South Florida Business Journal, *2015 Laureate* by Junior Achievement Business Hall of Fame, *Profiles in Leadership Honoree* by Leadership Broward, and *Influential Business Women* by South Florida Business Journal.

To contact Ginger Martin:

gingermartin@americannationalbank.com

4 Cylinder System to Social Media Success

By: Jacob Salem

"I fear not the man who has practiced 10,000 kicks once, but I fear the man who has practiced one kick 10,000 times."

- Bruce Lee

When I got out of college, I had a red 1993 Geo Prizm with a 4-cylinder engine. One thing I learned while driving a 4 cylinder, is that they're pretty slow, and if there is just one-cylinder misfiring, you're not going to go anywhere at all. However, if I kept the oil topped off, and the gas tank full, I could get anywhere within the continental USA in the most economical way possible. It was dependable and took me coast to coast multiple times. I lived in this car through a season of my life as I was figuring out what God had next for me. I think I took this verse quite too literal, "Go from your country, your people and your father's household to the land I will show you." (Genesis 12:1 NIV) I was driving around aimlessly while working on my master's degree in Divinity online. Through sunshine, rain, and snow, I knew that all I needed to do with my 4-cylinder engine was turn the key and go to the place He would show me.

Unbeknown to me, this season of brokenness and humility would be the cornerstone to my season of prosperity. As I traveled, I saturated my mind with the good, the pure, and the positive by listening to audiobook CDs and motivational tracks by people like Zig Ziglar, Les Brown, Rick Warren, and the complete Bible via "The Bible Experience." I still have my black leather-bound CD case that holds more monetary value within it than my Geo Prizm itself. Oh, and I still have the Geo Prizm as well.

After my travels subsided, I ended up back in Bourbonnais, Illinois where I completed my undergraduate degree in Religious Studies. My alma mater, Olivet Nazarene University had a program that provided ministry students the opportunity to travel and preach at churches in the representation of them. They did the prospecting, booking, and made all of our travel arrangements. The benefit to the school was that they were able to show the fruit of their teaching to multiple congregations while promoting their educational programs to future students. The benefit to me was that I was able to build a foundation for evangelism by getting my foot into multiple churches while acquiring the experience needed to preach the gospel in an effective way and allow the Holy Spirit to move the congregation to a salvation decision or reignite the fire of grace for those who had lost it. In short, my messages are this, "I am a sinner, condemned and unclean, in constant need of God's grace. As a former pharmacist without a license (drug dealer), if God's grace saved me, it can save you." The foundations of my ministry are Holiness, Righteousness, and Sanctification; and I believe that it is God's grace that empowers all three. I put a huge emphasis on Hope, Faith, and Love while using John 3:16 as my foundational scripture, "For this is how God loved the world: He gave His one and only Son, so

188

that everyone who believes in him will not perish but have eternal life."

Traveling as a full-time evangelist soon became very burdensome to me because many churches didn't have the budget to cover my expenses, and I felt very uncomfortable saying I needed an honorarium in order to bring God's word to their congregation. I was at a time in my life where I was living one love offering to the next (a love offering is when a church passes a basket to collect money for the visiting speaker as payment for their time) and knew that my entrepreneurial background needed to be put to better use. After all, we learn in the parable of the talents (Matthew 25:14-30) that if you do not use the gifts that God has given you, He will take them away. I began doing some research on how to put my speaking skills to other uses and found the Ziglar Legacy Certification program; a program offered by Ziglar, Inc. to become certified and authorized to train and present Zig Ziglar's most powerful presentations and methodologies. It was exactly what I was looking for, but there was one major problem: I was broke.

One hundred and fifteen thousand dollars in student loan debt, I faced the hard reality that I had no money, no reliable source of income, and my back was literally against the wall. In my black Carhartt coat with the hood up, I sat on the frozen hardwood floor inside my 600 sq. ft. rental home in the middle of a harsh Midwest winter with two brand new credit cards in my hand contemplating what to do next. Like Benaiah in 2 Samuel 23, I faced a lion in front of me and it was my time to fight. Although I had no logical reason to do it, I knew I needed to take a leap of faith, and use my very last dollar to cover the cost of my new venture, or I would forever be stuck in the endless cycle of trading time for money and living paycheck to paycheck.

The best part about jumping into a pit with a lion, is that there is no way out. The payment ran through and my spot was secure. My heart began to pound, and my palms began to sweat as the reality started to sink in about what just happened. I gave my very last dollar to attend a training program in Dallas, yet I had no means to get there and nowhere to stay once I arrived. In moments like this, your mind will choose fight or flight. I began writing down every thought that came to mind about how I could earn enough money to cover the cost of my upcoming trip. I could shovel driveways, sell drugs; oh wait, I gave that up to become a pastor, find a short-term gig on Craigslist, ask for donations, and the list went on and on. I decided to reach out to my friend and mentor, Tony Fight master of ONU. He and Craig Manes oversaw the Preaching Ambassador Program mentioned earlier and they were able to get me a rental car for the entire duration of my trip for only one dollar! Then, we were able to get me one more preaching opportunity and the love offering from that church was just enough to cover everything I needed.

At Ziglar, I met amazing people; I still call many of them family, even today. The training provided was exceptional and I was given the foundational tools I needed to achieve the success that I have today. I began building my online presence, prospecting with local companies, and was able to land my first sponsor; Laurie Kominek. She covered all the expenses for my first workshop. This was my first attempt at teaching "Building the Best YOU!" and truly, it failed miserably. The room was small, poorly lit, and I borrowed a rusty projector screen to show my slide show presentation. There were about 12 people in the room and all of them were family friends who only showed up for moral support, but it was an amazing learning experience.

Now that I believed it was hard to build a successful speaking and training career, I knew it was time to reach back out to Ziglar, Inc. for help. When I reached out to Tom Ziglar, I asked if there was anything, I could do to work alongside his organization to learn more about the industry. Even if the position was simply sweeping floors and cleaning toilets, I would do it with the utmost enthusiasm. A few months later Tom reached out with an idea that would change the trajectory of my life forever. He asked if I would be interested in being mentored by Billy Cox (a social media guru) and take over the daily content for the Zig Ziglar Facebook page with 1.2 million followers. He explained that most small businesses were missing out on social media marketing and that a Done For You Marketing Agency would be very successful. With mentorship by Billy Cox and my hard work, I would be able to build my own company as an independent contractor of Ziglar, Inc. and crack the code on how to turn 1.2 million followers into 1.2 million dollars and ultimately learn how to create generational wealth. As a relentless action-taker,

I got to work studying everything I could find about social media algorithms, best practices for modern-day marketing, and service offerings as a marketing agency. Simultaneously, as we solidified the agreement with Ziglar, Inc., I also closed an agreement with Toni Cooper, a Ziglar Legacy Certified Speaker as well. Those two accounts generated enough revenue to allow me to focus full time on honing my skills while building the business of my dreams.

On my journey to generating more wealth as a speaker, I built a business that has helped thousands of people implement a proven system for generating more revenue in their business. If you've ever failed in the past at building a business, it's not your fault. There's a lot of information out there, and it can be confusing. Many times, that information overload keeps you from success. It's okay. There are proven systems and scripts for success. You just need the right person to teach it to you.

"There's no secret to success, there's a system to success. Jacob Salem provides a systematic process that allows you to grow your business and allows your income to soar to new heights." - Les Brown

Here's what I've learned; social media is not meant to make you rich overnight, and there is a major difference between social media marketing and digital marketing. Social media marketing involves fluctuating platforms that are run by other companies who can change direction at any time. Digital marketing is something that can be created, owned, and operated exclusively by the business owner, and involves multiple mediums. (i.e. Social Media Marketing, Search Marketing, email Marketing). Using this knowledge, I've honed in on one kick and practiced it more than 10,000 times to develop the power needed to impact any industry.

I developed a four-cylinder marketing system that any small business owner, entrepreneur, speaker, trainer, coach, or marketing professional can learn and implement to generate an unlimited supply of their perfect customers, without wasting time or energy on things that simply don't work. The key is to build out all four cylinders in chronological order as I list them out below, and then allow all four cylinders to run simultaneously once complete.

The first cylinder is establishing social proof, or, as many refer to it, content marketing. Content marketing is the intersection of advertising and publishing. Let me explain what I mean. If you can generate enough attention toward your brand because of the value you are delivering, you can then advertise something for sale with confidence that someone will buy. Content marketing is essentially a free way to connect with your prospects and build rapport prior to ever meeting them. They then begin engaging with your content and sharing it with their friends. This social proof gives others those warm fuzzy feelings inside that make them believe that since other people know, like, and trust you, they can as well. When you begin creating content, you need to keep your ideal customer in mind. Where do they hang out, and what will they buy? When you know who your ideal customer is, where they hang out, and have committed to creating the content needed to entice them to engage with you, you'll need to create the bait (lead magnet) needed to turn that prospect into a lead. A lead is someone that was willing to give you their name, email, and phone number in exchange for something of extreme value to them. The perfect lead magnet is something that you give them freely to help them get from a before state to an after state in exchange for their contact information. The before state is the sad, depressed, or distraught state that someone is in while they seek out a solution for a specific problem in their life. The after state is the feeling they have after they implement your specific solution to their problem to help them achieve their desired end result. The key to a perfect Lead Magnet is that it must actually be consumed by your prospect and offer tremendous value within five minutes of the opt-in. If your lead magnet is too long or complex, you may lose your prospect forever, before you even had a chance to reach out.

After you create the perfect bait, cast it into the vast ocean of the world, and get a prospect on the line, you need to carefully reel them in. This is where you're going to begin nurturing Mr. or Mrs. Prospect, allowing them to learn more about you, your business, and your industry. There are multiple mediums in which you can nurture your prospects; automated email, automated text messaging, automated voicemails, automated messenger bots, and the list goes on and on. Email marketing is the most cost-effective marketing strategy and generates the highest ROI for businesses around the globe. However, email marketing has changed. In the 90's, email marketing had just begun, and people were getting a ninety percent open rate. Nowadays, there's so much junk coming across email, you need to make sure that your copy is written correctly and that your subject lines are scripted correctly, or you may end up in the spam folders. More importantly, you want to make sure that your emails deliver value, because if you're not delivering value your prospect will see you as a snake oil selling salesman and unsubscribe.

The last cylinder in our 4-cylinder system is the rocket fuel we use to scale businesses to exponential levels. We use paid advertising to drive traffic to social media platforms, landing pages, websites, and most importantly, lead magnets. Afterall, he or she who can spend the most to acquire a customer win! Paid advertising can make or break any business, but you can only guarantee your success with paid advertising when you avoid the hardship of trying every new thing that comes out and implement my one kick. You can skip the learning curve, build your audience faster, and generate more revenue in your business by simply creating social proof, a proven lead magnet, the proper nurture campaign to meet your prospect where they are, and persuade them to buy. Afterall, Zig Ziglar said it best, "If you believe your product or service can fulfill a true need, it's your moral obligation to sell it."

About Jacob Salem

Would you agree that everyone wants a taste of the good life: health, wealth, love, and happiness? Jacob Salem would, and he does everything he can to empower others to have it. This is the exact reason he has positioned himself among some of America's top motivators.

As the founder and Chief Executive Officer of EZMetrics, a global digital marketing agency who has represented some of the world's most foremost public professionals, speakers, and influencers such as Ziglar, Inc., Les Brown Enterprises, as well as several small businesses and non-profit organizations, Jacob has helped generate over 1,000,000 leads and prides himself on helping businesses grow and monetize their presence online.

Jacob has an uncanny ability to bridge the gap between high-tech and high touch so that businesses can embrace technology to gain trust in the marketplace without spending a fortune in the process.

Jacob is a follower of Jesus, a devoted husband, a dedicated father, and a passionate serial entrepreneur who has built his business on six foundational building blocks including faith, love, loyalty, character, honesty, and integrity. Along his journey, Jacob has learned what it takes to be happy, healthy, prosperous, and secure. It's given him better friendships, peace of mind, and hope for a better future.

It is his greatest joy to see others apply these same principles in their professional and personal life and watch it help them be more, do more, and have more than they ever thought possible.

To contact Jacob Salam:

Jacob@EZMetrics.com

Tele. (810) 955-9804

Website: www.EZMetrics.com

DECISIONS

By: Catrese Kilgore

It was 7:30 pm, Kamry was still at work, as usual. Spreadsheets were on both computer screens; papers were strewn across the desk. Her shoes were kicked off next to her chair as she sat with her head in her hands trying to hold back tears. She never thought this day would come, but here it was, and in a couple of hours she was going to have to make one of the hardest decisions in her life. She was finally ready to quit the job she had worked so hard to get and thought she would never leave. Hard decisions should have been easy for her by now. Her life had been filled with hard decisions. She sighed and thought about the first hard decision she had to make. That decision changed her life, but also saved her life.

Kamry was born and raised in St. Louis, Missouri but relocated to Houston, Texas at the age of nine with her family. Her mother left her biological father after repeated years of cocaine abuse and overall neglect when she was 11-years-old. Their divorce was final right after her twelfth birthday. Most kids would be sad about their family splitting up, but she and her sisters were actually happy. They had a very dysfunctional family, so they welcomed change. It was obvious their Mom and Dad no longer loved each other and that they were only making each other miserable. Therefore, as children they were just as eager as their mother for a divorce from their father. The sad part was - they didn't know what was coming as a replacement.

198

During the summer of 1986, between her 6th and 7th grade school years, her mother met a man named David. After being in a bad marriage for over twenty years, her mother was thrilled to have met a man, and spent the entire summer living with him in his apartment. Kamry was twelve, her oldest sister, Kaela was 19, her sister in between the two of them, Kate, was seventeen, and their baby sister, Kriss was five. That summer was very fun for Kamry. She had no guidance, stayed out late every night, spent nights at friends and was barely at home. She got into trouble, did things she shouldn't have, but all the while wondered when her Mom was coming home.

In August, the week before school was to start back, Kamry's Mom came home, but not alone. She brought David, her new boyfriend, to move-in with their family. David was twenty-nine years old, nine years younger than her 38-year-old mother.

Within one month of David moving in, he had had multiple fights with Kamry's two older sisters, Kaela and Kate and ending up kicking them out of the house all together in early October. So now it was just her, her little sister, Kriss, and her Mom. Kamry felt extremely isolated from her two older sisters. She was alone; her two older sisters had always been her protectors. Now with David in the house she knew she needed protection more than ever because she now had a newfound sense of fear. She just didn't know exactly what she needed protection from. She would find out about three months later when David's real agenda became known.

It was January 1987, Kamry had gone to bed a little late after watching her favorite TV show, The Cosby Show. She woke up around 3:00 am and was extremely confused. She knew something was going on but had no idea what. Was she dreaming? Where was she? She opened her eyes and realized she wasn't dreaming. She was in her room. It was dark but she saw the familiar movie posters on her wall confirming she was in her room. Kamry lay there and thought, "What woke me up? Why do I feel weird?" Just then she noticed her sheets moving and realized she was not alone. Someone was under the covers with her. All she could think was, "what the hell was really going on?"

David was in her bed, under her covers, doing something that her 13-year-old brain couldn't process. Kamry tried to move away but she was pinned. She immediately felt a hand on her mouth and another one on her neck. She tried to scream but could barely breathe, let alone scream. Was this a nightmare? Yes, a nightmare coming true.

As David held his hand over her mouth and squeezed her neck, he could see the fear in her eyes but didn't stop. He asked her, "If I remove my hands do you promise to be quiet?" Kamry didn't answer, she couldn't talk. He then threatened her and said "If you scream, I promise I will kill you, your mom and your little sister. So, are you going to be quiet?" Kamry slowly nodded her head in agreement as she felt the tears fall down the creases of her eyes to the bed. That's when he explained to her that he had always had an attraction for young girls. He said it like it was a normal thing. This was years before the #METOO movement, years before Surviving R Kelly so she had actually never heard of this but knew it had to be a major sickness. She was a 13-year-old little girl. All she wanted was for her Mom to come save her, but she wouldn't and couldn't scream. She just cried and begged to be left alone. However, David didn't stop. Kamry closed her eyes and tried to imagine she was somewhere else while he continued to molest her. After about 10 minutes of pure agony for Kamry, he was done.

The next morning Kamry could barely look at her mother. She felt dirty and guilty. Had she caused this? In reflection, David's moving in was classic pedophile behavior. A younger man moves in with an older woman with four daughters, no sons, no brothers around, or any other males who could get in his way. This had been his plan all along.

Kamry had to make a decision. Should she tell her mom? David had threatened to kill her, her mom, and her little sister if she told. She decided to say nothing that day. Maybe she could just avoid him, and it would go away. That worked for about three days.

It was Thursday evening and her mother had to go to her night school class. She begged her mom to take her with her, but she didn't. Instead Kamry was left at home alone, with David. She spent the next two hours being chased around the house. She locked herself in the bathroom and thought she would be safe. Kamry sat there crying, pleading to God to help her when she saw the door knob coming off. David was unscrewing the knob. No one was there to help her. He came in the bathroom and molested Kamry again. That time it lasted about thirty minutes. Once it was done, she was allowed to go back upstairs to her room - in tears again. That's when she decided she was telling her mother no matter the consequences.

That Friday after school, she found her mother alone. She looked so happy that Kamry immediately got sad, knowing she was going to take this happiness away.

"Mom, David has been touching me. He came in my room at night and has been cornering me and touching me in the house." The words just sat there. Her mom looked at her but didn't say a word. She then said, "What did you just say?" Kamry repeated it and waited again. Her mother's response was not what she expected. She said, "You must be mistaken. Why would you lie like that? I know you don't like him since he kicked your sister out, but he would never do anything like that. HE is a good man." Kamry pleaded with her mother to believe her. Her mother said she would talk to him. Kamry thought, finally David will be out of here.

That Sunday morning, her Mom woke Kamry up at 7:30 am and basically started an inquisition. She sat her down next to David and said, "Tell me exactly what happened." David glared at Kamry with major disgust and disdain as if she was the devil Kamry knew he was. He of course denied everything, even requesting to take a polygraph test. Kamry thought, "Wow, did he really think he could pass a lie-detector test. I know what happened. How could my Mom even believe him? Why would she even question me? Who was this woman? When was she going to kick him out of our house?"

Her Mom asked did she want to call the police. She then said if the police came, they would take Kamry and her little sister to a foster home until they could figure it out. Kamry's fear of the unknown was worse than her fear of David so she said, "No, don't involve the police." Her mother took that as a sign that nothing really happened.

The next week passed by slowly. Kamry went to school every day and tried to act normal. The family ate dinner at night and tried to act normal. Kamry barely slept because she didn't want to be surprised. That weekend she asked her mom what she planned on doing and her mom said, "I don't know what to do. He says he didn't do anything to you, and I love him. I finally want some happiness of my own."

Did that mean Kamry was the sacrifice for her mother's happiness? WOW. The next day Kamry's mother bought a deadbolt lock for her bedroom door that couldn't be opened from the outside; even though she didn't "actually believe" anything had happened. At least Kamry could sleep at night. David still caught her at times outside of her room, but it was very rare. He then started physically abusing her since he couldn't sexually abuse her. She dealt with it and that became her new normal for a whole year.

It was February 6, 1988, a colder than usual grey Saturday morning. The grass was brown, the day was cloudy and grey. Kamry was sitting on her twin bed in her room. She loved this room, first time ever she actually loved her room. She had decorated the room with movie posters from Kate's job. Kate had the coolest job ever, she worked at a video rental store and so she got all the best promotion posters from the movies and Kamry had them plastered on her wall. Even though her furniture was at least 20 years old (it had been her Moms, then both her older sisters), she thought it was awesome. Her mom had custom painted it grey with pink trim and her curtains and bed spread were pink and grey.

Everything was so nice for a 15-year-old girl, except the bolt lock on the door. However, over the last year that bolt lock was Kamry's best friend and protector. She often checked to make sure it was locked anytime she was in her room just to be sure she was safe. She never went to sleep without it being locked. This morning, it was locked.

As she sat there thinking about what clothes she would throw on for the day, she heard screaming and immediately flinched with fear. Screaming wasn't unusual for their household and it was typically followed by some type of violence so Kamry had formed post traumatic distress to any loud talking. Screaming and violence was the norm, just not usually this early in the morning. Cartoons were still on for goodness sake. "What is HE yelling about now? Please don't let it be about me."

Everyone was still at home. That included her now forty-one-year-old mother, her 20-year-old sister, Kate who had just moved back in the house, her eight-year-old sister Kriss, and David, and David's eighteen-year-old nephew, Geno who also was staying with us. Kamry opened her bedroom door and ventured down the hall closer to the noise. It was coming from her mom's bedroom. She slowly peaked her head around the corner and saw David strangling her mother. Her mom's eyes were filled with fear. He had finally snapped, and she was his target. David saw me standing there and said, "You are next". He must have eased up on her mom's neck a bit because she gasped for air and said, "Get out of the house, go run!" Kamry immediately turned and ran to Kriss' room. Both Kate and Kriss were there and she told them they had to go now. They were all in their night clothes, but it didn't matter. The three girls jumped up and headed to the door downstairs with David right on our heels. Kamry looked back and saw he had a butcher knife in his hand while her mom was trying to hold him back. He really was going to kill them. Just then Geno grabbed David and held him. He held him long enough for all three of the girls to get out the house and run to their neighbor's house for safety. That was the last time Kamry ever slept in that house. She was about to be an adult at fifteen. She had to take care of herself because it was clear her mother would not.

The plane was almost in St. Louis. It had been such a long day, such a long 2 days for that matter. But all Kamry could think about was what lay ahead. It hurt too much to think about what all she had left in Houston, not knowing when or if she would ever return. She had made the tough decision to leave. She held back the tears looking out the airplane window. She felt like the air was extra dense because she could barely breathe. She could hear her heart pounding deep in her chest as she clutched her fingers and winced. Her head was ringing from the headache that was only getting worse.

Kamry was 15 years old and about to start a whole new life without her mother or her three sisters she had spent her entire life with until then. How did she end up making this choice to leave? It took her two and half years to finally do it and there was no going back. She couldn't give up on her dreams for her own life and staying in her mother's home would have destroyed her. She made the decision to live, to fight another day. She had dreams, she didn't know her destiny, but she had dreams of being successful, wealthy, and proud of her accomplishments. Her life had a purpose and David wouldn't stop that. She envisioned herself fulfilled and happy but didn't know how she would get there. As the plane descended into St. Louis, she thought about the quote that would end up being her mantra and carry her through life - *"Never give up, for that is just the place and time that the tide will turn."-Harriet Beecher Stowe*

About Catrese Kilgore

 Catrese Kilgore is independent Certified Public Accountant. She specializes in financial due diligence, financial and tax implications of complex transactions, mergers and acquisitions, public and private company audits, initial public offerings, employee benefit plan audits, and process improvement projects.

Catrese is currently the Chapter President for NABA Houston, and a member of the Houston United Way Women's Leadership Council. In addition, she is a frequent speaker on professional development and diversity topics and has served as a continued education instructor for numerous accounting and auditing courses.

She graduated from the University of Missouri in 2003 and earned her Certified Public Accountant in 2004. She is married to Henry Kilgore and they have three children, Cydney, Kelsey, and Chase.

To contact Catrese Kilgore:

Email: Catrese.kilgore@gmail.com

Tele: (630) 240-5500

Finally Figured Out What I Want To Do With My Life… Now What?!

Thought Inward Then Energy Outward

By: Sean Mullervy

Office Space

Two decades ago, I was extremely frustrated with my life. I wanted to make changes but didn't know how. So, I learned how. Then, I faced fear and adversity. After I conquered them, I became unstoppable.

Prior to age 25, I never knew what I wanted to be when I grew up. My childhood dream was to play basketball in the NBA, but I knew that I needed a more realistic goal. In high school, I was in the accelerated program and graduated near the top of my class. In college, I was in the honors program and earned an academic scholarship. Although I got good grades, I didn't love any of my courses. I couldn't decide on a major and declared a general one when I was forced to. Like many high school and college graduates find, attending school didn't reveal my vocation. Maybe my first "real job" would?

For the few years up to and including 1999 when the movie was released, I lived the cult classic *Office Space*. I was the main character Peter Gibbons; my manager was the supporting character Bill Lumbergh and the rest of my coworkers rounded out the cast.

The cubicle neighborhood, inane conversations and "TPS reports" were eerily similar.

Naively, I thought that I would find success and happiness simply by working for a big company. However, I soon realized that I was in a dead-end job and mind-numbing environment with zero-chance of finding anything. Like many recent college graduates find, my first job didn't reveal my vocation. Maybe a part-time graduate program would

Although I got great grades, I still didn't love any of my courses. Even grad school didn't reveal my vocation. Maybe a full-time doctoral program would? Stop! I was a pretty smart kid, but smarts and schools weren't enough. I badly wanted, no needed, to find the career that best fit me. Time to try a different approach.

One of my many jobs during undergrad was a bookstore clerk. Somewhere in the bookstore, I hoped was the answer. It was! These are the 3 books that changed my life…

1. Discover What You're Best At, by Linda Gale
2. Do What You Are, by Paul Tieger & Barbara Barron-Tieger
3. Do What You Love, The Money Will Follow, by Marsha Sinetar

First, I determined my aptitudes. Second, I determined my personality type. Third, I discovered my passions. After some research, I found the best "vocation combination" for me. It was an amazing feeling!

The vocation was Financial Advisor. It perfectly combined my passions to help people, educate them and make their lives better. I got those from my father who was a teacher and administrator in our hometown's public schools. It also perfectly matched my half-extrovert/half-introvert personality. I liked talking to anyone anywhere about anything which worked well for sales and marketing, but I also liked analyzing numbers behind the scenes which worked well for planning and investing.

Now, I knew my calling. Soon, I would be calling.

Gladiator

Fast forward to early 2000 and I'm a 26-year-old, first-year financial advisor. I didn't have any money and didn't know anyone who had any money. Not a good combination. The company paid me an $18,000 draw on commission which was even worse than the $24,000 salary I just left. With the decrease in income I had to decrease my expenses, so I moved back home with Mom and Dad. The professional wardrobe I could afford to buy consisted of only: 3 suits, 6 shirts, 12 ties, 1 watch, 1 belt and 1 pair of shoes.

This job had goals and deadlines. If I didn't acquire 5 or more planning clients (i.e. individuals or couples) in the first 10 weeks, I would be immediately terminated. If I didn't acquire 25 or more planning clients in the first 52 weeks, I would probably be terminated. This job had no participation trophies.

My "office" was a recently cleaned-out broom closet with no window and a solid door. Also, I had to share it! My office mate's desk was so close to mine that we couldn't open our drawers at the same time. Occasionally, people walking by our open door would laugh at us. All we had on our desks were: pens, pads, phones, White Pages and paper leads from the company.

Most of the leads given to us first-year advisors were, shall I say, interesting. Some of the leads were recent and qualified, but the others were what management called "refreshed". Those leads were old and recycled from former advisors or from current advisors who gave up on them. Those prospects had been called by multiple advisors dozens of times over the previous few years. Management often told us that "A lead is a lead is a lead." and "They're so old they're new."

Back in those days, financial advisor success rates were terrible. Because of the bull market in the 1990's, a lot of people tried to become an advisor then found out quickly how hard it was. For new advisors, it was a sales job first and advising job second. Most advisors at other firms failed within the first year and most of those survivors failed within a couple more. The planning firm I chose had the best first-year program in financial services at the time with outstanding training and support. Even with that, many of my firm's advisors failed within the first year and many of the survivors failed within a couple more.

One of my favorite movies is the award-winning *Gladiator*. A few months before it was released in mid-2000, my mentality was the same as the main character Maximus. I had a dream, was prepared to fight, would not be defeated and would eventually earn my freedom. Gladiators had an unconquerable will to stay alive and built resilience to achieve victory. Alas, I knew that many of my comrades would die in battle.

To sum up my life at the time, I had: no money or connections, a shared closet for an office, a stack of old leads and a phone. In addition, I was starting a business from scratch in an industry with a very low probability of success. Awesome! When I told my friends what I was doing, they thought I was crazy. Facing thousands of phone calls, hundreds of meetings and countless rejections over the next few years, I went back to the bookstore. These are the 3 books that saved my life...

1. As A Man Thinketh, by James Allen
2. Think And Grow Rich, by Napoleon Hill
3. How To Win Friends And Influence People, by Dale Carnegie

First, I realized that I'm the sum of my thoughts. Second, I learned how successful people had directed their thoughts. Third, I learned how to communicate more effectively. After some research, I created a business plan. I was ready to enter the Colosseum!

Up to this point, I had done a lot of reading and thinking inward. After this point, I would need to transmit massive amounts of energy outward.

Like most things in life, success as a first-year advisor was a numbers game. Before the "Do Not Call List", it was a phone calling game. My firm's weekly goals were: 400 dials, 100 talk-tos, 30 conversations, 10 appointments scheduled, 3 appointments held, and 1 client acquired. To make that formula potentially work, one had to smile and dial on the front-end.

Management gave me and my 2 dozen classmates flip books with scripts, and we had 30 minutes of calling "role plays" before each 2-3 hour "phone clinic". Even after inspirational motivation and constructive criticism, many of my classmates just weren't driven enough to do the activity or strong enough to deal with the rejection. During phone clinics, I could hear down the hall many of them talking negatively and a few crying occasionally. Some of them constantly went to the bathroom or outside for smoke breaks to avoid the pain. Some would call family and friends so it would sound like they were having conversations to managers walking the hall and look like they were making dials on the phone records.

One by one over my first year, old and new classmates resigned or vanished."This is too hard." and "This will never work." were common utterances from failing and failed advisors. They felt pressure from the goals and adversity then panicked. Each time someone quit, thoughts of quitting and fears of failure crept in to my mind and heart. So, I morphed them in to beliefs and emotions of success. "This is hard, but it will work." and "Think long-term, not short-term." was what I told myself. As opposed to my quitter colleagues, I got excited about the goals and adversity then focused. Basically, I learned to love the grind.

Every day, I'd wake up determined to succeed. I arrived at the office by 8:30 a.m. before classes started at 9:00 a.m. and stayed until 8:30 p.m. after the required 8:00 p.m. That added 1 hour of work to each weekday. Lunch was from 12:00 to 1:00. Some of my classmates would leave the office early and return from a restaurant late. Not me. I went to the gym next door from 12:05 to 12:50, ate a power bar at 12:55 and was energized for the next 7.5 hours. Saturday's required time was 9:00 to 12:00, but I skipped lunch and stayed until 3:00. Those 3 hours plus the 5 from weekdays added a full 8-hour workday to my week.

Every class, I'd take copious notes and listen to the instruction versus just hearing it. Every phone clinic, I wouldn't leave my desk and would call only prospects. When I saw first-year advisors not putting in the work, I'd avoid them and hang out with the ones who were. When I had opportunities to hang out with veteran advisors, I jumped at those chances to learn from them.

Because mirroring success is much easier than reinventing the wheel, I compiled strategies from veteran advisors for each cold call

214

scenario. Busy signal? Would call back within 15-30 minutes. No answer? Wrote down the time and would try again at another time in 1-2 days. Answering machine? Left a professional message then tickled out a call for a different time 2-3 days later. Hang up? Called right back (Those were my favorites). Not interested? Started a conversation. Yelled at? Still started a conversation. Objections? Handled them. Interested? Booked an appointment. I made over 500 dials before booking my first appointment and remember that conversation to this day. Once I gained confidence from the repetitions and added personality to the conversations, appointments started coming in bunches.

Within my first 10 weeks, I acquired 5 planning clients and went from temporarily to officially hired. The fifth client was acquired with only a few days left before my potential termination date. The combined relief and exhilaration from beating the buzzer still ranks as one of the best feelings in my entire life. Within my first 52 weeks, I acquired a total of 40 planning clients and finished second the region. In my second year, another region promoted me to management. Outside of my parents, most of the other clients that I acquired in my first year were sourced from cold calls. The remaining clients were referred to me by a few of those cold-called clients.

Now, all of those prospects didn't just show up to my office and sign up for financial plans. I had to meet with them for 1-2 hours and overcome: numerous objections, a lack of experience, a limited wardrobe, 20-something looks and reverse age discrimination. Most of the prospective clients were 2-3 times older than me and had sons or grandsons my age. When it came to handling people's money, the perception of older advisor as better advisor often became a prospect's reality. Luckily for me, I was always more mature than my age and an excellent listener.

Interestingly enough, a good number of those prospects told me in person that their family or others didn't listen to them much anymore. I did and it wasn't just for the potential business. I genuinely enjoyed listening to their stories and learning about them. To paraphrase a collection of similar quotes, true wisdom is learning from other people's mistakes and successes. I have based many things on personal advice from previous generations.

Over the past 20 years as a Financial Advisor, I've turned plenty of setbacks in to setups. Over the next 20, I'll probably have to turn plenty more. The following paragraph contains some of the basic principles that I learned while building and growing my business.

Business isn't fair. Life isn't fair. Get over it! There's no entitlement in sales. There's no crying in sales. Save the drama for your momma! You don't deserve anything that you don't earn. Failure to earn something is your fault, not anyone else's. Don't blame others or your circumstances! Success is an equal opportunity employer. It doesn't care who you are or where you came from. Stop whining and complaining, have a goal and a plan then work hard and smart! Fear lurks in the shadows. Adversity is around every corner. Take both of them head-on! My first advisor manager was an officer in the U.S. Marines. Improvise, adapt and overcome. Observe then attack! My first office building didn't have a room where I could hide from my responsibilities, pet puppy dogs and lick ice cream cones while everything outside would magically become OK. Activity, activity and more activity. Realize that anything is possible!

I figured out what I wanted to do with my life then didn't let anything or anyone (including myself) stop me. I thought then I did. My passion became my purpose and profession. Those were all key. I was emotional about my passion but didn't get emotional during my adversity. That was the key.

Rome wasn't built in a day and my changes took years. Success takes patience. I've engaged well over 10,000 investors in conversation and have learned something from every one of them. Experience takes time.

Today, I'm living my dream. I love what I do and don't feel that I work. Being a financial planner and manager comes naturally to me. After transitioning from an employee advisor to an independent advisor, I can provide a higher level of service and greater selection of products to my clients. I now own a thriving business with many long-time clients and most of my new clients are referrals from existing clients or other professionals. My cold calling days are long gone. Most importantly, I have the honor of helping people and improving lives.

The word "unstoppable" is an adjective. One definition is "Cannot be stopped from continuing or developing.". I constantly improve my professional knowledge through formal training. Using that definition, I'm still unstoppable.

About Sean Mullervy

 Sean Mullervy, MBA, CFP® is an independent financial advisor and small business owner who is passionate about helping people achieve their goals and realize their dreams. Sean has been a member of numerous organizations in the Greater Fort Lauderdale area and had his own show "Dollars & Sense" on Money Talk Radio in South Florida. When Sean is not helping people, he enjoys his other passions: sports, music, dining and traveling.

Sean wrote this chapter about his personal experiences of inspiration and perspiration to make similar life changes easier for other people. He dedicated this chapter to the wonderful women in his life, wife Janet and mother Louise, and the gentleman who set a great example for him, late father Dennis. For more information about and to connect with Sean, please visit his website and social media profiles…

To Contact Sean Mullervy:

SeanMullervy.com

Facebook.com/SeanMullervy

LinkedIn.com/in/SeanMullervy

Twitter.com/SeanMullervy

A REAL ESTATE OF MIND

By: Raymond Meinhardt

Did you know that the majority of people that become real estate agents will be out of the industry within three years? Even more shocking: fifty percent of new agents will be out of the real estate business within the first year. Why are these statistics so shocking? What causes someone to get into what I consider to be one of the greatest professions in North America and maybe the world only to drop out within one to three years?

To be a successful real estate agent, one must learn many new skills and be thorough to use these skills on a consistent basis. It is the process of real estate. I believe that when a person gets into real estate with a fixed mindset, and the process of real estate gets too hard, it is easier to drop out of the business saying "real estate is just not for me" rather than pressing in and working through the tough challenges.

Someone entering real estate with a growth mindset, on the other hand, sees the challenges and embraces them as an opportunity to grow and to become more professional, more successful. Even when the challenges are great - and they sometimes are - the agent with a growth mindset tackles it from different angles or sometimes reaches out for help. A growth mindset is not threatened by a greater need for effort. For the successful real estate agent effort is not an indicator of an insufficient amount of a fixed ability. For the successful real estate agent effort is seen as a necessity to produce the desired results.

Your mindset is what is going on in your head at a given moment about a particular person, a situation, or a particular thing that you're encountering. Your mental response to a situation—that's your mindset. Now mindsets are either very positive or negative. The question is, how do you control it, manage it, and operate it? How do you keep your mindset working in your favor every single day? Here are a series of points I want you to follow, implement, and take action on to strengthen your mindset.

1. Always be honest with yourself where your skills are so you can develop the mental strength to win on a daily basis.

What skills do you have that are carrying you forward and building your business and what skills are you lacking that you need assistance with? Be honest with yourself, your broker, and your coach, if you have one. We tend to develop the skills that we feel the most comfortable with versus the skills that lead us in the best direction to doing our business. We can develop mental strength if we develop strong skills. Knowledge equals confidence, ignorance equals fear. As our knowledge increases, our confidence goes up. On the other side, if we are not confident our whole ability to take action decreases. What we want to work on consistently is the mental strength to accomplish the goals you've set.

2. Strong people, not necessarily the best producers. I'm going to define strong people as those who set goals and achieve those goals.

Why, because they eliminate the option called failure. Failure's not part of their terminology. I'll often ask some people to spell "failure." Their response is, "I don't know how to spell failure because I don't participate." The mental capacity and the mental strength to eliminate failure from your day-to-day life is critical. While prospecting its of certainty that you will be told no? And it is almost also certain that you're going to have sellers reject what you have to say. But only you can decide what your response is going to be to those types of rejections. The option of most agents is to take the path of least resistance, which agents do every day and they eliminate failure by not talking to people. They buy their leads off the internet because it's easier. They hold an open house so no one will be offended when they walk in the door because they're not going to offend them to ask them to buy it. We can eliminate failure by not taking action.

We can instigate failure by taking action if we take enough action, so you're going to win, yes. Therefore, the failures don't make any difference.

3. We have to have an absolute unwavering desire to achieve the goals we've set in spite of the ups and downs of this crazy business.

The nice part about real estate is you get a good lead, you're excited. You call them and they are not interested, you're depressed. You get a great listing, you're excited. It never sells, your depressed. You have a great buyer appointment that's prequalified and ready to go, you are excited. They don't show up, you are depressed. This is called the life of a real estate agent. It's just part of the process so one of the ways to really get through the ups and downs is to have that outright desire. What is the goal you have set for the year? How many listings, sales, closings, how much income? If you focus on that, then you'll have the mental capacity to do your job.

4. If you develop a strong mindset, you remove some of the drama that this business creates.

This business called real estate creates a lot of drama. Real estate creates a lot of drama and as long as you are subject to letting that drama run your life, you're never going to have the mindset necessary.

5. Both our personal and business environments are critical to controlling and keeping a positive mindset.

The people you hang out with, your associations and your peers. Are they positive, and are they strong? Are they always going to be the kind that encourage? Are you going to encourage the people that you're around? Are you or can you be positive and strong?

The environment we keep, is it a positive or negative one? If you we're asked the following question what would be your response? Do you spend a lot of time individually talking to people? Would you answer that most people are not very positive, and you don't want that influence in your life? If you were asked why do you have to be very strong and positive? Would you answer be that it is my role, my job? If you were asked how to control the daily environment, you operate in. Would your answer be I'm not going to read the newspaper or watch the news, I'm not going to go through most of what people do every day because most of what people do every day really can be upsetting, create emotion and drama?

Starting to see how It's all mindset?

6. We become like the people we associate with. To develop a strong mindset, you have to be more particular.

Be careful who you hang out with and you can strengthen your mindset. It's critical we keep expanding our minds and expanding our mindset while strengthening our mindset. How do we do that? **Mindset, Skills, Activities, Action.**

The mindset of a can versus I can't. The mindset of a can versus I won't. The skills knowing what to do what to say. The activities which you and I both know require a lot of work to be involved in actions that lead to listings, and sales on a weekly and monthly basis. You have to focus on taking action every day. Hopefully, I will be able to get you to incorporate a lot of them into your subconscious mind, and get you using them in your day to day work.

Remember that real estate is like a blue sky. There are no limits in terms of what you can achieve in this business. No one is doing it to you, no one is doing it for you. You decide how far you want to go. You get your head in the right place. You must be clear about what you want. You must believe in your abilities to achieve your goals. You must be committed no matter what. You must connect to what is most important to you on a daily basis. For me it's by the grace of God and all His glory every day, that I am able to work in the best industry in the world. I am so blessed to truly love what I do every day.

Remember your results are the by-produce of your mindset, strategies, actions, habits, routines and efforts.

About Raymond Meinhardt

Raymond Meinhardt is a financial real estate advisor, mentor and coach to many of the most successful real estate and mortgage professionals throughout the US. Having been a part of hundreds of millions of dollar deals in both the real estate and mortgage industry, Raymond Meinhardt has been recognized as one of the leading advisors and investing authorities.

His mission is to provide the most complete, accurate and unbiased real estate advisory information. His education and training materials, the latest cutting-edge tools, and strategies and the very best coaching and mentoring services available has changed the lives of hundreds.

Starting from very humble beginnings, once homeless, and at one point living on the streets of Santa Barbra, Raymond rose to top of the real estate world by following the guidance of top mentors himself.

The name of his company, "Hi Impact Business Coaching," describes the essence of what Raymond Meinhardt is all about. He considers having a mentor to be the secret to success in any endeavor and truly believes that every real estate entrepreneur has the ability to become financially free given the right mentoring relationship and tools to do so. Hence the name "Hi Impact Business Coaching".

For more information you can reach out to Raymond at

To **Contact Raymond Meinhardt:**

RMeinhardt@outlook.com

Facebook.com/RaymondMeinhardt

Linkedin.com/RaymondMeinhardt

or check out his website at:

www. HiImpactBusinessCoach.com

www.YourRealEstateofMind.com

Healing From Within: My Journey Back To Life

By: Dr. Elaine Cruz-Abril

Imagine waking up every day exhausted, with no idea how it feels to just, "feel good." Imagine living with the belief system that every cell of your body is your enemy, that you came into this world to struggle, and that, long story short, you are broken. I know that if you knew me today, you'd never think this was me.

Since I remember, I have memory flashes of the day that I was born, being in the cold sterile environment of the hospital in my mother's arms. I remember feeling her unconditional love as well as her pain. My mother got pregnant with me in the middle of a major depression, after her dad passed away. He died May 6, 1986 and I was born a year after, May 7, 1987. **Synchronicities…** As you can imagine, her pregnancy and delivery, was very difficult. Not only did she lose her dad with whom she was very close to, but also the love of her life. My father was an alcoholic and she was a single mom to my older brother. My brother and father didn't get along which worsened the situation and on top of that she had to take care of a sick difficult child. I suffered from chronic asthma, severe allergies, chronic pneumonia, bronchitis, hiatal hernia, acid reflux, chronic gastritis, chronic constipation and during my teenage years I also suffered from anxiety and depression. **When I was 3 years old, my mom, ran away from my dad for our safety and** we never saw him again. **She loves to tell me stories on how rebellious and angry I was with her for "abandoning" my dad. Needless to say,** it was a difficult time for our family, and I didn't make it any easier **since losing my father was very trying.**

There are experiences in life where we create belief systems that do not serve us. "Knowing" that I was broken unwanted and with no possibility of healing, **I created the belief that** my only option was to suck it up, be strong and push through the pain. **My mother was always in pain. She suffered her whole life from chronic depression, fibromyalgia and many other health conditions. But as a single mom, she pushed through and raised us on her own. She couldn't keep a job for too long because it always came down to choosing between her job or taking care of us. When I was around 9 years old, we lost our home since my mom couldn't pay the mortgage. We became nomads, sleeping wherever we could for many years.**

I remember, one morning when I was 12 years old, staying by a bus stop with my mother, my little sister with nowhere to go. We were homeless. Feelings of frustration, humiliation and powerlessness overwhelmed me. I remember my mom would tell us, "Don't worry everything is going to be fine." But I angrily thought to myself, "There is nothing fine about this situation… We are good people… How could God be so unfair with us?" It was that day at the bus stop that I made a promise to myself; to never depend on anyone for anything. If things are going to change, it was up to me. So, I decided to do something about it and started working to help my family move forward. I took it upon myself to never allow anything like that to happen ever again.

From middle school to college, I studied during the day and worked late nights. I would barely sleep, because of my breathing issues and the medication I was taking. I felt so exhausted, drained and just tired of living. When I was 15 years old, I dropped out of school because my body couldn't continue with the load and life became all about working and supporting my family. My mom and sister tried to get me to go back to school or at least finish the exams to pass the school year, but I would not have it. I was overtaken by depression, my body and soul felt drained, and I just needed to rest but didn't have the time. Nevertheless, thanks to their unconditional love, I motivated myself to finish the exams, passed the year and went back to school.

During this time the hospital was my second home. We always had our "emergency backpack" ready to go. Every doctor and nurse knew me by name, and I would be asked, "Elainesita otra vez aqui?!" It was very normal for me to be in and out of the emergency room on a regular basis and to be hospitalized at least once a year. Sometimes I would spend up to 3 months in the hospital. I was dependent on 4-6 different medications and a breathing unit. I could never run, play sports and even though I was an A+ student, I lost years of schooling because of my health and my recurrent hospitalizations.

My last hospitalization occurred when I was 18 years old and I remained in inpatient care for almost 3 months which resulted in losing my first semester of classes in college. Right after I was discharged from the hospital, I met my life partner, David. He was a very happy, charming, active and so full of energy. He would always invite me to work out because he loves healthy living. He couldn't believe that I was unable to perform any strenuous physical activity. On the outside, I "looked" very healthy. I was a skinny, good looking girl so nobody could tell that I was struggling big time with my health. One day, David convinced me to go for a run and not even a minute into it I had an asthma attack. He then learned that I was being serious.

After a couple of years dating, he noticed that I was struggling with neck pain. He asked me to visit his chiropractor since he had amazing results. After I started with Chiropractic my neck pain went away but the most impressive thing was that I also started to notice other changes. My allergies were decreasing in frequency and intensity, my digestive issues improved, and I wasn't having asthma attacks anymore. People would tell me that I looked happier, less explosive, not as angry and in general, more relaxed. Also, I notice I was sleeping better and waking up with energy, to the point that I started working out. All these changes got me thinking about what I was doing differently and the only thing I could come up with was that I was getting adjusted. The doctor I was seeing never told that chiropractic could help with all my other health challenges, so it was a big surprise experiencing all the healing that was happening. I was so fascinated by my healing that I encouraged David to become a chiropractor. It was very exciting to have my own personal chiropractor 24/7!

We decided to move to the United States so he would study chiropractic and I would pursue my dream of becoming a "big time" lawyer. While researching chiropractic schools for him I continued learning about chiropractic and it's vitalistic philosophy of life. The more I learned about chiropractic, the less interested I was in becoming an attorney. **Until one day, while listening to a chiropractor giving a talk, I had an "aha" moment and I heard a clear voice in my head saying, "you should be a chiropractor." Immediately, I called my mom to share with her my epiphany. She was very surprised at first and questioned my motives by reminding me how much I hated chemistry, math and the sciences that I was surely to encounter in my curriculum. Nonetheless, I was so confident in my decision that this was the path for me. I remember laughing and telling her "I know what I'm doing, don't worry about it". After hearing my conviction, she supported me 100% and was so excited because she too would have her own personal chiropractor!**

I can share with certainty that chiropractic adjustments changed my health, but it was the chiropractic philosophy that changed my life. The understanding that my body was not my enemy, that I was not broken and that I had a lot of potential for healing. That our bodies are a self-regulating, self-healing organism and that under the right conditions have the ability to heal themselves. Real healing only comes from within so we must create the environment through our daily choices. Everything we think, feel, eat, drink and put into our bodies affects our internal chemistry and nervous system. Through chiropractic I gained a sense of purpose, a sense of giving for the sake of giving, a moral responsibility for service and a love for sharing my story to bring hope while guiding people to transform their lives. Sharing your story might be difficult, but you'll never know who will get inspired by it, if you don't share it. Like BJ Palmer the developer of chiropractic said: We never know how far reaching something we may think, say or do today will affect the lives of millions tomorrow.

The first step in the healing process is stepping out of "the victim role" and taking responsibility for your life and your health. We must own the concept that we are creators of our own reality and extinguish the belief that life just happens to us. As we start making the right choices, we become more responsible and our sense of awareness, influence and power grows. All throughout my life I had to learn not only to become responsible about my own life but also about my health. It was the struggles that I had to endure that showed me the lessons I needed to take my power back.

There is a **life force** that runs and regulates our bodies through the nervous system. **In the Hindu philosophy it's called prana and in the Chinese philosophy they call it chi.** In chiropractic we call it innate intelligence. **This intelligence** organizes, balances and governs every single function in our body. Every chemical reaction, every tissue formation, and every immune response is controlled and coordinated by this **innate intelligence** which operates through the neurological system. Every living thing has an **innate intelligence. On this topic, Deepak Chopra states "There is no fixed physical reality, no single perception of the world, just numerous ways of interpreting world views as dictated by one's nervous system and the specific environment of our planetary existence". It is through our senses, controlled by the nervous system that we perceived "reality". The brain generates and sends electrical signals through our spinal cord and nerves to every single cell, organ and tissue in the body.** When there's interference in our nervous system it will affect how we adapt to life and the stressors from the environment.

As human beings, we experience stressors daily. There are **three main** types of stress that affect **how our nervous system functions**: physical, chemical and emotional. If the body cannot fully adapt to these stressors, a cascade of incoordination can develop, particularly if there's interference with the expression of innate intelligence. I can tell you, looking back at my life, that my nervous system was not working appropriately **which impeded the full manifestation of my innate intelligence. For many years I tried to be in control of everything, being a type A personality, working so hard to get the outcomes I wanted that I would force things to my detriment.** As I started my healing journey, **I'd discovered that one of the reasons why I was so sick, and life**

234

was so difficult was because I was subluxated. Today we know that all the stressors a woman experiences through her pregnancy has the potential to affect the baby's development and health. Probably since the moment I was born, I was subluxated. My mom's difficult pregnancy, being born as a C-section baby, unhealthly eating, all the medications and the emotional stress I was going through while growing up are some of the reasons why I struggled with my health. However, my body was trying to make the best with what it had, and symptoms are a way of our bodies telling us to stop what we are doing and pay attention. My body was trying to tell me something. **When an experience (physical, chemical or emotional) isn't fully integrated it becomes stagnant and it's stored in our body as potential energy. A subluxation is potential energy stuck in our bodies that creates interreference in our nervous system. Since our neurology controls everything in our bodies, being subluxated affects everything. The chiropractic adjustment facilitates the healing process by releasing the tension on the nervous system and converting that potential energy into kinetic energy, the energy of movement and healing. We are truly beings of light, tone, energy and vibration, radiating our very own energy signature. When we get adjusted, we vibrate at a different frequency, our nervous system comes out of a vigilant sympathetic dominant state, resulting in a greater state of awareness, ease and focus.**

Subluxations and symptoms often indicate the necessity of change and transformation in our lives. The more refine and

235

connected is our nervous system, the more in tune we are with ourselves. Our level of awareness increases, and now we can really listen to what our body is trying to say when it whispers. The more we listen, the less it will have to scream.

Healing is a process, it's never linear, it has several up's and down's and more importantly it requires time. My healing process took years. However, through the process of getting adjusted I created more awareness, connection and ease. I transformed my lifestyle completely. I had to change from being reactive about my health and wanting to suppress the symptom to being proactive and finding out what the root cause was. I learned to listen carefully to my body and intuition. I became more conscious of who I was, what I was doing, thinking, eating and who I was being. Now I make myself a priority through self-care, understanding that everything is connected, and that I am the most important thing in this world. As I became less subluxated I was able to reach my fullest potential and start expressing a higher vibrational frequency. I quickly experienced that by expressing myself in this manner, a clear resonance rippled out into the world surrounding all life and making little changes for the growth of mankind.

I'm eternally grateful for my journey and everything I have been through because it made me who I am. My journey has given me strength, compassion and the tools necessary to inspire and facilitate healing to the people I serve. It is with absolute certainty in my personal power that I now transform the lives and wellness of my patients.

About Elaine Cruz

Dr. Elaine Cruz Abril is an Author, Public Speaker, and Healer who owns and operates a successful vitalistic chiropractic office, Express Life Family Chiropractic, located in Fort Lauderdale, Florida.

She was born and raised in Puerto Rico where she graduated Magna Cum Laude with a bachelor's degree in journalism from the University of Puerto Rico. Having experienced many physical challenges herself, she found in chiropractic a catalyst that transformed her life which then inspired her to become a chiropractor with her life partner, Dr. David Lopez. She completed her Doctor of Chiropractic degree Magna Cum Laude from Life University in Marietta, Georgia. She is passionate about inspiring and transforming people's lives so they can live the fullest and best expression of themselves.

Dr. Elaine is the co-creator of the ADIO Self Care Retreats, with the mission of holding space and empowering women to find themselves in life. She also serves as an advisor to Chiropractic Worldwide Missions, an organization co-created by Dr. David Lopez that helps people with limited resources to achieve a greater state of health thorough chiropractic around the world. Dr. Elaine is a board member of the Women's Council at the Greater Fort Lauderdale Chamber of Commerce.

Dr. Elaine loves to share with her family and friends, travel, practice Yoga and CrossFit, dance and go to the beach with Dr. David and their two doggies, Mister Fu and Princess Leia.

To Connect with Dr. Elaine Cruz Abril :

https://www.expresslifechiro.com

Recognize Temptation from Trials

By: Jovanna Martinez

"No man is an island; no man stands alone "…**John Donne,**

To understand this quote, you must understand my back story, which is neither a typical nor a tragic story. My life journey has been one of overcoming, aspiring in spite of adversity and fulfilling calling.

Calling the Unqualified

Successful women who reach their goals makeup a small percentage from those who attain them. Anyone looking at my life from the outside in, might want to know how I accomplished these accolades. It's been made clear to me by those who supported my dreams saw a grace that was only visible to those with eyes to see.

It's been difficult at times being qualified; through my life experiences. However; it has been those trials and temptations that have shaped my character. The truth is those called are typically unqualified and then God qualifies them.

In the story of King David (1 Samuel 17:23-24) we learn that David's brothers were trained to be warriors; while the youngest, David was but a shepherd boy. As a shepherd, David perfected his protective skills that included use of a slingshot and stones to kill predators (lions, bears etc.). When the Israelites are threatened by

240

Goliath the giant, who does God call to defend, David, who in all eyes was unqualified, but who defeats Goliath with one blow.

Some experience the, "comparison syndrome" in life. I know I've asked; "Why my friends life seem much better than my own, they're financially stable, a loving family with a father and mother? Why did she/he get the better position and not me etc." I wonder if King David felt the same about his family. His family and the Israelite army seemed stronger, more capable than him. Yet, David developed skills in his daily routine and grew in his trust in The Lord and this ultimately gave all he needed to get the job done. Through life's routine, we are being shaped for what's to come.

My Life at A Glance

At 3 years of age my parents divorced, and my grandparents became our full-time caretakers. They immigrated from Cuba with nothing other than their personal dreams. Their new dream quickly shifted to parenting in their mid-sixties in the midst of language barriers and financial struggles. They never shared words of encouragement, affirmation or the importance of education, from what I remember. They loved and cared for our needs the best they could. Although, grateful it never replaced the need for my parents.

My mom lived with us for a while until I was about seven. I loved my mom without really understanding her role, albeit, I always somehow felt a connection to her. I admired the way she would do her make-up, get dressed up to go out with her friends and exercise in front of the TV with the VHS videos. Her outfits were funny but at times I would jump in and try to join her exercise routine. It wasn't perfect, but it was enough to love her.

Our relationship would become more distance when my mom decided to move out of her parents' home in favor of living alone. She said to me, "I am just moving, but I will come visit often and call daily." She did for a while but as her life became more involved away from the daily responsibilities of being a parent (her parents picked up the slack) the regular calls and visits stopped. She became an absent parent just like my dad, who had moved away to California, where he remarried into his culture (Pakistani) and started a new family. I have memory that my mom would pick us up on the weekend, take us to the county fair, beach, movies and the flea market etc. Although she did try it was never the same or enough. I never experienced a real deep meaningful conversation with my mom growing up.

Now adults my brothers and I sometimes speak about the time, when our mother invited us to her home for a Thanksgiving dinner. After dinner, we argued, as you would expect from teenagers and siblings. She was expecting appreciation for her grand gesture, but instead, her kids were out of control and lacked discipline. So, what did she do? She shipped us back to our grandparents' home in a taxi. I should mention I was only ten and it was not the norm to send your children unsupervised on a 30 min. cab drive. This memory is humorous to us now.

A Father to the Fatherless

"When my father and my mother forsake me, then the Lord will take me up."
Psalm 27:10 (KJV)

Having to face absentee parents, my brothers and I couldn't find solace within ourselves, because we were only one year apart in age. We all experienced pain differently and none of us really had the experience to hold safe space for the other. We all suffered a huge sense of a void inside, but my rescue came through a real and present relationship with an amazing, unconditional and loving Father.

When I was eight, my uncle had recently had his own encounter with Christ and shared it with the family. He invited us to a local church in Miami; and my heart knew I wanted it All. All that God had to offer. No hesitation, it just made sense, so I ran to the altar and gave my heart to the Lord. This decision made at eight changed how I began to do life. In my darkest hours, I learned that I could cry out to my Father and He answered. I unlocked the unknown treasures, the core to my very existence, building a foundation with truth, love, character and having God the Father as my guide. I could now recognize right from wrong. It was truly a discerning gift that would surely be tested by life's trials and temptations as the years progressed.

Trials Produce a Joy

Trails $\rightarrow$ Testing of our Faith

In scripture we learn how trials produce joy through the testing of our faith (James 1:2-8).

Believe it or not to have a trial in your life is truly a gift from a loving Father. We are not exempt from experiencing suffering, pain and/ or sadness in different seasons of our lives. This is necessary in order to trust, surrender, build character and optimally test our faith and draw us near to our Creator. We can now shift our minds and heart to a Creator/Artist that promises to produce the award-winning peace of art. Joy!

Trails are out of our control; What we can control, is our Attitude and Response towards the trials.

Personal Trails

My mother's absence was a difficult season, it led me to experience a great deal of sadness and pain. I cried out to God to hold me and asked Him why this had to happen to me? My friends seemed happy with their family. I wanted the same. I trusted God that He had my best interest. His response did not come right away but years later.

In time, I learned things about my mom that God had protected an impressionable girl from. My mother was not a Christian, and she was into heavy witchcraft and other worldly things. Can you imagine if I lived with her full time? I could have been confused and dragged into her darkness. This is a perfect example of *how* *'God works for the good of those who love him..." Romans 8:28 (NIV)*

I would pray for my mom regularly and she has surrendered her heart to the same loving Father that has protected me all these years. My heavenly Father also works on restoration. This came when my mom invited my brothers and I as adults to her home for lunch to ask for our forgiveness for her actions and abandonment. It went well no cab ride was required.

My father, is Pakistani, making me a CuPack. Yes, my mom fell in love (or she thought) with someone opposite to her own culture and beliefs, a Muslim Pakistani. At 11, I packed up my bags and made the decision to visit my father in California, but unbeknown to me, his entire family had moved to Karachi, Pakistan. That's right you read this correctly, my father shipped me off to Pakistan for several months so that I could be inducted into my paternal heritage, which meant becoming Muslim. Four years into my father's dream of his daughter becoming his Muslim princess, we reached a crossroad, I'm asked to remove my cross necklace as an example to my younger siblings, but because I could not do it, I'm shipped back to my Cuban family in Miami.

My father to this day does not understand how a 14-year-old could not move away from the foundation of the cross, to which she ran to at age eight. As a teen, I knew there was much more to my relationship with Christ, rather than just a prophet, as it was often discussed and viewed in the Muslim religion. My father is a loving and caring man, who we pray for often. He now lives in Tampa, Florida. In 2018, we enjoyed Thanksgiving dinner together with the entire family.

As a teenager, after 4 years away, reconnecting with my brothers and grandparents was not easy. Things were not the same it felt different. I was much older & there were new rules and expectation. My brothers and I couldn't find common ground. I remember, them telling the neighborhood kids that if they saw me on the front porch to run right in, otherwise they were at risk of being evangelized for Christ. In high school, kids would call me "Holy Jovy." This didn't bother me; I was excited to come back where I could worship freely. A contrast from my father's home. In less than a year, I became independent after finishing high school and working. In this season, I learned that in order to live a life of purpose, abundance, and fullness, I had to plunge into the living Word. I was not your typical kid, but my amour to this day, has protected, convicted and equipped me to discern temptation from trials.

Early Influence on Business Success

As a business owner, I learned what sometimes what appears to be a good opportunity, may in fact be the root of a trial. At the time it may seem unfair but hold steadfast for the fruit.

When I left the pharmaceutical industry and ventured into the mobile ultrasound/ diagnostic industry, initially I sought out a partner. The partner appeared honorable and of integrity. However, as our business grew, the partnership was challenged, and this individual broke agreement. This trial allowed me to test my Faith, because if I stayed, I'd be guaranteed 50% income, but his breach of trust was not okay. Without knowing what the outcome would be, we trusted in God's promises and took the leap to go on our own. The decision meant starting from the ground up. We needed equipment, and we didn't even have financing or knowledge if we could qualify. But I knew that an unevenly yoked partnership wasn't honoring to God and therefore would not be fruitful. Had I not taken the leap, we would never have realized the successful business I now own and operate with my husband of 18 years.

"Blessed is the man who remains steadfast under trial, for when he has stood the test, he will receive the crown of life, which God has promised to those who love him." (James 1:2-12 ESV)

The Derailment by Temptation

Temptation → Sin, Pulls Away from God's Will

God loves us, I experienced His love first hand during my trials, but He is not going to approve bad behavior (sin). Just like any good parent, He wants the best for His children. He knows that making bad choices can cause painful consequences. As an example; if you have a child in high school as I do, we push them to do their best because those grades will follow them. If they perform poorly, they may not be able to enter their desired college. Some kids just can't see that far in advance. God is the same, He just loves us so much and knows that temptation will lead to sin and will have bad consequences and even physical and/or spiritual death.

Good and loving parents don't want their children to lie, cheat, steal, get drunk, harm themselves and not learn how to distinguish from right and wrong. Our heavenly Father has the same desire for us. Doesn't that make sense? My eyes were opened when I learned in the Word, to discern trails from temptation.

"Let no one say when he is tempted, I am being tempted by God; for God cannot be tempted by evil, and He Himself does not tempt anyone. But each one is tempted when he is carried away and enticed by his own lust. Then when lust has conceived, it gives birth to sin; and when sin is accomplished, it brings forth death. Do not be deceived, my beloved brethren..." James 1:13-16. (NIV)

It may seem harsh to speak so boldly but when we talk about temptation God is very clear and it's a complete contrast from trails. Trails produce joy; however, temptation can lead to death and separation from the Father. Jesus was led to temptation by Satan, but Jesus prevailed over temptation to fulfill God's plan, to connect us back with the Father.

"Now the deeds of the flesh are evident, which are: immorality, impurity, sensuality, idolatry, sorcery, enmities, strife, jealousy, outbursts of anger, disputes, dissensions, factions, envying, drunkenness, carousing, and things like these, of which I forewarn you, just as I have forewarned you, that those who

practice such things will not inherit the kingdom of God. Galatians 5:19-21 (NASB)

Pursuit of temptation derails the plan God has laid out for us before we were born. However, we all fall short, but when we have control over it, through recognition of wrong choices, it leads us to regain reconciliation and redemption through the sanctification of the blood of Christ. We should consider the practice of sin and the condition of our hearts which leads, to call to action "Repentance."

There is hope in Truth; it's not how we fall; it's how fast can we ask for forgiveness and restrain from that current sin/temptation. *"For though the righteous fall seven times, they rise again, but the wicked stumble when calamity strikes." Proverbs 24:16 (NIV)*

One of the hardest seasons of my life, occurred over a ten years span, after I left college and begun to open my life to worldly living (all things that separate us from God's truth). I stopped going to church regularly, reading the Word and connecting with likeminded people. I put God on the back burner.

I would realize later how those ten years would be fundamental for growth and maturity to what was to come years after… I had no excuse I felt His shadow from the distance. I knew He was calling me to be alert, but I chose to give into temptations. Giving into temptations stunted my potential growth, because I opened myself up to fears, thoughts and circumstances that I had never experienced before. It's similar to the experience of Eve in the creation story, she was given all knowledge and abundance but was forbidden from eating one fruit. She was tempted and took a bite, which changed the trajectory for mankind. We now suffer pain, which had never been known before.

~Temptation is within our control. The key is to understand that the choice to pursue temptation always has detrimental consequences and will stunt your growth. God has given us what we need in His Word to avoid temptation.

How to Put Feet to Action

All truth diverts back to the righteous Truth inspired by God. You may have imitators writing portions of truth to give themselves the glory. However, the reality of right and wrong has been passed on for decades. For example, what I am revealing comes from my heart, but it originated from a Truth that's biblical.

- Ask God; "help me to understand your ways". (James 4:2-3)
- Ask God for what you need and want but do so with the right motives (James 4:2-3)
- Ask God for wisdom (James 1:5)

God wants an intimate relationship with us, built on truth; with motives that are pleasing and aligned with His will. He is the authority. As a child I knew I lacked the role of my parent. My search to fill the void my parents left, led me to authority over my life in God the Father.

Believing in an all knowing, all present God, met that I would have to come clean; be honest about my actions, when in contrast to the Word. When I chose temptation, I didn't justify it as being okay. And, He knows the condition of our heart. He looks to change us through trials and wants us to avoid temptation. Therefore, I try to just come clean remembering; He loves me exactly where I am at; with the hopes that I will move out of sin/temptation.

My friend Patricia always says; "We need to love people where they're at".

He loves us where we are at; still sinning but no longer a Sinner. Working through sin, temptation, bad habits and restoring one's heart through his Truth and the Holy Spirit. He starts from the inside, the core-heart, thoughts desires and convictions. Although, I had a supernatural experience, at a young age; people all over the world have similar experiences. God transforms the heart at any age.

God's promise to us, "Being confident of this, that he who began a good work in you will carry it on to completion until the day of Christ Jesus." Philippians 1:6 (NIV)

About Jovanna Martinez

 Jovanna E. Martinez, a successful mobile diagnostic business owner and entrepreneur, is a dedicated wife, mother and philanthropist with a heart to serve. Mrs. Martinez possesses a bachelor's degree in Business and over the last several years was an impactful agent as a marketing and sales representative for several leading medical health service and pharmaceutical companies in the United States, managing and developing multimillion-dollar books of business.

Mrs. Martinez expressed that it was her great pleasure to share and take the reader through a journey that will instill hope, encouragement and help navigate through temptations and trials that will shape any person's life. She stated that she had been given the opportunity to experience the many trials that come with the roles of a wife, mother of two boys, a business owner, building relationships with family and friends. And that through all these roles she found that it shaped her heart, mind and soul.

Mrs. Martinez would like to extend gratitude first to my Lord for allowing amazing people to enter her life, her church leaders, amazing friends and their families, coworkers, office manager/clients and business owners that saw God's favor in her life and opened opportunities to shape her success path.

To Connect with Jovanna Martinez:

info@onsiteimaging.net   Onsiteimaging.net   1(888) 265-8670

MISSING LIMB SENSATION

A Father's Mission to Rescue His Sons

By: Mark Robbins

First grader Avielle Richman was six years old when she was taken from us. She was a victim of the Sandy Hook school shooting. Her father couldn't endure the agony. He described the loss of his daughter as similar to the experience of missing limb sensation. Not phantom pain... but real pain. Pain with unbearable intensity. Pain without mercy. Pain with anger. With no relief in sight. Avielle's father took his own life. This tragedy was reported internationally.

I, twice in my life, experienced intense loss of my adopted twin boys. Thankfully the outcome was not the same as Avielle's father, but I would describe it as the igniting of an unrelenting passion that has consumed me to this day. Only now, it is what fuels my existence and purpose to advocate for the voiceless.

I experienced my traumatic separations from my adoptive sons, as something similar to a missing limb sensation. The first incision occurred in a custody situation that resulted in my children being taken 700 miles away from me. This cut was deep. A crushing emptiness set in, but I knew were my boys were located, but in the moment felt helpless.

Living on the Atlantic coast, I could not pass the beach without reminiscing about dipping my toddlers' toes in the ocean's foam. The art projects of my children remained plastered on my walls. I would hear a child say "daddy" in the grocery store and I'd swear my kids were in the next aisle. I knew that I couldn't bear the longing for my missing toddlers, so I did what I could and moved the 700 miles to Pennsylvania to once again be a hands-on father to my children. This was no easy feat, as my ex-spouse at the time and I were in a significant storm. Divorce is a difficult experience, but when there are children involved the pain is exponentially compounded. Through this experience I was taught the value of selflessness and I was able to employ all the strength and skills that I knew I had, but had forgotten to engage in while lost in the depths of my emotional turmoil.

The next incision tore through scar tissue and resurfaced my missing limb sensation. It occurred under the strangest of circumstances. My boys now 19, and had grown and enjoyed each other for several years. We decided to return to the beach. The pain of the custody battle was long past and my relationship with my ex-wife was healed. What amazed me was how the acute pain that incisions and yet heal over time. The scar is a reminder of the emotional ground I covered. My twins were now living near me as college students and I was able to return to the beach with them once again.

In 2017, in search of further self-improvement and learning, my boys and I signed up for a workshop. Quickly, after we started the program, I began to notice ominous signs. The workshop's intent was to promote volunteerism, while concurrently adding value to adults seeking personal growth, prosperity and a greater appreciation for life, others and community. But what must be understood is that at this time in my life, I had become extremely interested in research, advocacy and in particular justice.

After involvement in the program I learned of incongruences in the way the business was run, as compared to my beliefs and passion for anti-corruption. I started digging, and my findings served to prove my hypothesis, that the program was not all above board. This in and of itself did not sit well with me, because I have dedicated the better part of the last several years towards advocating for the underdog, those without a voice, many times to my own detriment. But this time was different, as the scalpel making the incision was plunged deeper, I noticed that my own children were being indoctrinated into the culture of the organization and they were once again being moved (although not physical) further and further away from me, as their father.

I employed my skills and past experience to do what I could to figure out a strategic plan. I researched the program and others that were similar. In particular, due to a recent influx of news and information at the time on domestic human trafficking, I quickly shifted to explore, if this program was an organized cult-like operation, in some way associated with this criminal enterprise. Human Trafficking takes on many different appearances in the community. It is a 300-million-dollar industry. The victims and the perpetrators are not 'typical' rather they present sometimes as well intentioned, prominent and professional (people least likely to be suspected).

From research I found that the definition of a cult is quite simple. It involves students being captive to *(1) religious veneration* and *(2) devotion granted to the owner/leader.* The program I had involved my family met these criteria resoundingly. The mantra, *"Being responsible for everything all the time,"* I felt was a convenient way for the group to distance itself from responsibility. It siphoned attention and activity inwards and did not address the contradictions of competing wills and differing manifestations. Based on my findings, I believe that unwittingly, my kids and I joined a cult at a minimal and potentially a trafficking racket.

After we spent 14-hour days immersed in the pursuit of euphoria, experiencing sleep deprivation what I learned later, was that we were systematically developing trauma bonds capped with love bonding. The love bonding was always present at the end of the workshop so we could ride the tide of togetherness into the costly next phase. An "us versus them" mentality took hold. Euphoria is sneaky. It keeps secrets. Euphoria neglects to tell its hosts that it serves temporarily. From within this organization, what was confusing at the time, was the power differentials created.

Ironically, I was deemed a leader within our class – described as a "powerhouse." And it was these leadership qualities that ultimately served as the organization's greatest antagonist, when I realized what was occurring in my relationships with my boys. I

256

was asked to leave the organization, due to my persistency in finding out more, but my kids were retained, effectively, as chattel. My exit from the environment was used to create fear in others, who could be contemplating the same action. When I realized what I had just gone through and that my boys were still entrapped, I called on the help of my wife and co-parent. Together we wrote specific letters to seek our boys' release, but we were taunted by the knowledge that our kids were legally adults. The pain of missing limb syndrome became unbearable, excruciating and unrelenting.

It was then that I realized that exploitation of vulnerability is real, and that it is these vulnerable blind spots that provide the access perpetrators need to brainwash and coarse. The methods from the outside looking in are devious, measured, strategic, insidious and ensnaring. Psychological bonds result in dehumanization. And worst of all – they worked. I understood repressive leaders – from Jim Jones to David Koresh – who when studied were diagnosed as sociopaths, with a diseased sense of self-worth, who operate with a lack of conscience. Sociopaths possess counterfeit confidence masquerading as charisma. And people buy it.

This time my suffering came from the torment of knowing my boys were entrapped behind a curtain of evil, and one that I had freely walked into. This realization, coupled with the reality that my adoption of my twins – on just 12 hours' notice – was a miracle, was overwhelming. I vowed to do everything within my power to eradicate this ugly transition for my kids because it was not to be our final chapter.

Each day that passed, we grew further apart. At my wit's end, I decided that the liberation of my children would entail taking down Goliath. The dismantling of the organization became my "unstoppable journey." Using my pointed and acerbic writing style within my blog, I surgically exposed the group's illegal tactics and informed others that they had rights and instilled hope that they could achieve their goals. The result of my unrelenting crusade was that the organization lost following, released several members, and we got the attention of national new media. You would have thought this was sufficient to regain my boys' freedom. It wasn't. The psychological bonds were deep, and I then I uncovered another layer of corruption and abuse.

Those susceptible to yet another organization presenting itself under the veil of benevolence and virtue, were young transgender adults seeking full self-identified gender transition surgery. This organization was allegedly running a full-service surgical recovery center that offered, "top" (breast) and "bottom" surgery. The sex trafficking ring lured young biological females from around the world who curiously travelled alone and were asked not to bring cash nor rent a car. The victims were under the pretense that they'd receive the complete transition surgery, comfort pets, lifelong friends, and delightful excursions. The "extras" were attempts to groom the youth with the goal to traffic them in the sex trade. My son came out as transgender and he was entangled even further.

To my horror, I learned that the youth who received the "top" surgeries were used as a part of the business façade. Their shirtless pictures were posted on a public web site to have the nonprofit appear legitimate. The local kids were the likely candidates for "top" surgery to include the royal treatment the nonprofit advertised. Their alleged satisfaction was touted to enhance the organization's reputation within the region. Dreadfully, the kids flying in from overseas weren't so lucky. They were exploited. They were invisible to the outside world and had no one looking for them. After arrival to the U.S., nothing prevented these innocents from being directly trafficked as they surrendered their passports and were whisked away in the luxury van. Their fate was sealed at this point. The ingenious design fooled everyone for years. As my son became prey this deeper layer of corruption, I fought to find a way to both meet his need for understanding and acceptance, while furthering my investigation of the very organization(s) that was most supportive of him at the time.

The balance to maintain my relationship with my boys as open as possible, while concurrently continuing my efforts to unmask what I believed to be a sex trafficking ring was done in a highly disciplined manner; the same discipline that led to my achievements in academics, athletics, and my finance career. Contrary to popular belief, the most powerful confirmation of an actuality is not the witness of a single episode, but rather accumulating evidence (red flags) to such a degree that a conclusion can be reached with certainty. I dusted off my "Probability and Statistics" book and went to work. My first red flag was the knowledge that same day surgery requires no recovery. And ultimately, I revealed over 75 red flags that could not be ignored.

My exposure of the collective groups (and the leaders intersecting within each) led to my kids' freedom, as the parties involved viewed us as liabilities. My children were jettisoned but many others were not so lucky. I know of people who lost their lives, families and significant relationships, not to mention the loss of humanity that ensued, which can never be measured.

It is important to point out that the strength of brainwashing and creating trauma bonds relies on shared pain. My boys and I to this day continue to work our way through the pain of being separated, coerced and entrapped, by well organized, seemingly well-intentioned people, who in fact were fronts for the fast-growing organized criminal enterprise in the US – human trafficking. Today, my boys and I continue to purse our passion to ensure that others do not fall prey to the same tricks we did, and I'm working on a bill that will provide measures for restitution for victims of this social injustice that is also a public health issue.

These are a few of the red flags that one should look out for when joining organizations from my experiences:

- Unlicensed insiders (risk- safety laws and basic dignities are circumvented)

- Wide latitude is given to the trainers,

- Exercises that are horrifying and intrusive, (one I lived through was supposed to be a cathartic exercise, but it was so intense that vomit bags were offered. Another exercise had us identify the least attractive person and to tell them what made them so. Yet another exercise involved critically pointing out the worst personality traits in others in terms of how they "showed up." I knew one gentleman who had early onset dementia. This poor man was told that he was dead to the world and broken in spirit. This was part of the trauma bonding. Bear in mind, the agenda was not to heal but to break.

- Inhibitions to be void of value (The reality is that inhibitions are natural, good, and God given. They serve as social lubricants for a civil society. Destroying them does not make the world a better place),

- Encouraging drug use; to promote relapses and chemical highs are encouraged. In the program I attended, there was a student, who was clearly in need of medical detox. She died of a heroin overdose after "graduating." Multiple students suffered drug relapses. One student committed suicide. He took a swan dive off a highway overpass after ingesting the opiate-mirroring substance called kratom – a cult favorite. Kava stores selling the highly addictive kratom were heavily owned, managed, and supported by the cult members.

- Misuse of private information to threaten and further create fear; I experienced private information being used against me when I left. In fact, I was forced to answer personal questions as part of a four-hour deposition used to intimidate me. A sham restraining order was filed against me and I was banned from the property, to separate me physically from my boys. Social media was used to shame me.

- Use of humiliation – The most grievous manipulation of my twins occurred when I was separated from them and they were told to be spoon fed by older adults in the organization. The given reason? So that my kids would "receive the love that they never received from their father."

Another facet of my experience that is also shared by many who have survived trafficking is that law enforcement is not very helpful. I sought assistance from law enforcement during my attempts to free my boys from the entrapment but found little help. In fact, my experience was quite the contrary.

A bright Sunday afternoon as I sat in my car before a malfunctioned RR crossing, being a good Samaritan, I helped drivers through the crossing by raising the wooden cross bar.

Months later and coincidentally after I pressed into my investigation, I was shaken by police pounding on my door. I was arrested for a felony, jailed, and had my mug shot taken for the paper. I was charged with interfering with a RR operation (that wasn't operating). After the shock, I examined the police report and noticed a slew of inaccuracies. Based on my findings and not willing to back down, all charges were eventually dropped.

I cannot prove it, but sadly, sex trafficking best operates as a network – as racketeering. There is too much money to be made with almost a zero per cent conviction rate. Now that I have been reunified with my boys and we are all doing well, but not without extensive cost personally and financially, I have turned my passion into my purpose. My plan to introduce legislation that will hold the consumers of sex trafficked victims responsible for restitution/compensation and rehabilitation costs is underway.

I have learned that to fight for those we love, who find themselves without a voice, being exploited, means that sometimes we stand alone against the wind; against momentum expanding exponentially. The people who supposedly love us, now turn against us. But, to be unstoppable, these experiences built in me a resilience to persevere, particularly in difficult circumstances.

My biggest goal has been achieved. I have my kids back in my life. Through the traumatic processes we've lived through, the outcome is that my children and I are closer – but I shudder to think how close I was to losing them. My kids and I agree that this was "an experience we're glad to have lived but it is something we would not want to happen again." My transgender child is transitioning on schedule and we maintain a very close relationship. I am grateful that my kids were able to witness the love I have for them based upon my actions to rescue them. This is a memory they will hold dear. One that I hope every vulnerable person entrapped in trafficking is able to experience. It requires substantial resilience to be an unstoppable Warrior!

About Mark Robbins

Mark Robbins has a diverse history. As a "seeker" he had been involved in many different groups which include The Pentecostal church, New Age and the Unity Church, the Mormon Church, and Eastern thought and teachings. Some major life hurts have also equipped Mark with empathy, compassion, philanthropy, and a high sense of justice.

As a kid growing up, Mark was a stellar athlete based more on determination and will than natural talent. No one worked harder than Mark. It is this side of Mark that propels him forward as an activist. Mark has published a blog with more than 11 million-page views, and he seeks justice for victims in the same way he has approached all of his life endeavors.

Mark earned an MBA at Lehigh University where he graduated at the top of his class. He previously graduated from Wake Forest with a BA in Economics. Mark expanded his business acumen by passing the four exams required for a CMA (Certified management Accountant) and the four required for a CFM (Certified Financial Manager). He has owned a medical device company and a wellness chain. He also spent years in in senior corporate finance and has worked at a company that evaluated business models for IPO's.

Mark lives in south Florida near his twin kids (age 21) and with his Maltese named "Killer." He has taken on anti sex trafficking as his passion.

To reach Mark email him at MarkRobbins3000@gmail.com

UNSTOPPABLE = PERSEVERANCE

By: Viviana Malamud

Completing an action over and over again until it is better. Someone who perseveres will look to achieve their goals, by using their intelligence and positive attitude. Because of perseverance we can achieve lasting meaningful goals.

From the bottom ground to getting up standing tall BECOMING PROUD

It is a long journey; it is not an easy one

It is a satisfactory road

It is a blessing to be alive

The moment is enjoyable

The thought is positive

The feeling is love

The actions are good and tender

The compromise is TRUST

Trust in You

Believe in You

And never forget to also give yourself LOVE

I recently viewed a short video on the topic of human beings being useless, yet still loved. I automatically related the subject matter to a special need's child, a handicapped partner and a very old family member. The video ends with this wisdom: The subject in the video is told, "You are good for nothing, but I do not know how to live without you."

The high intentional meaning is you are loved even in the worst of your circumstances. You are unconditionally loved. That is when the other person discovers your true meaning, your true self, regardless of what you can or cannot do or give.

Some years ago, I found myself in a situation where my true value was not appreciated. A dear friend reminded me, of this situation and asked me how I felt then. I remember the pain, yet I did not allow myself to suffer it. I neither kept negative thoughts in my head nor did I keep any resentment for too long. Shortly after my father died, I assumed a CEO Position in our family-owned business, but I felt I knew nothing about the role. Now I can share that I quickly learned our business needs, and although it felt like a long road, I've been able to maintain my father's wonderful legacy.

The foundation that he left, under my care not only provided financial stability, but also an emotional legacy that included an important set of values applied to how we run our business. We all learned from him and have honored and felt very strongly about these moral business practices. The business, the physical building and everything inside of it, to me was and still is how I continue to feel close to my father. Having said that, and the fact that I come from a social work background not a business or financial one, my attachment to the business was purely EMOTIONAL.

My brothers feared that my management of the business from an emotional attachment could detrimentally impact our fiscal bottom line. Therefore, they made substantial decisions about our business model and then charged me with the responsibility of creating the operational framework in our business setting. What this involved was an introduction to a new CEO option, and a new vision for the business. The expectation was that I was supposed to stay somewhat involved since it was the role I had taken on, but it left me thinking, "There is no need for me here, what am I supposed to be doing, if another person will be CEO? This initially led me to feel completely useless, helpless, fearful, and frozen.

This new situation paralleled exactly what I observed and what was described in the video I recently watched on being devalued and unconditionally loved. I was feeling USELESS, yet my family still loved me unconditionally. Of course, I did not know it or feel that I understood this at the time. At the time, the experience caused me to shut down, to "put my mind in a box", I could not see beyond my current circumstance. I was hurt, I was frustrated, feeling so useless and helpless, ashamed and fearful. In fact, I would freeze every time I had to see my brothers. Each encounter with them was another painful moment of uncertainty.

It was after these repeated experiences that I began to gain clarity and understanding. I told myself, "If I don't like what I am experiencing, I need to change my view of it, my attitude, my perception of it. My reality was my perception of it, it was not reality. I was the problem therefore I am the solution. In my eyes I was seen as a useless human being. Yet I was being loved as a sister just like I had been my whole life." Why could I not see that, at the time.

From one perspective my brothers were taking care of the business, to ensure we all could survive financially (this meant taking me out of the administration area) while concurrently still loving me unconditionally. It turned out that they did not kick me out, even though I totally felt like they did. In fact, these series of events that gave rise to so many ugly thoughts and feelings inside of me, turned out to be THE learning experiences that probably my father was hoping for me. It led me to turn around and pick myself up again with force of perseverance, responsibility, justice, enthusiasm, discipline, honesty and strength.

Through the experience, I learned so much about myself and how much stronger I could really be. How much more I still need to learn. How much more I still can do and overcome. And over time I continue to become a much better version of myself.

Today and every day, I am so grateful not only to my parents, my children, the Universe, my friends, and everyone I encounter each day, but also to my brothers for what they taught me through that difficult business experience, that actually created the greatest stepping stones and learnings in my life. I have gained so much insight and wisdom. I changed my perception of things and this led to many realizations in consciousness and enhanced awareness. Today, I have even more appreciation and a better understanding of the value of myself, others and the identities we assume in life, and most important, I feel loved.

BELIEVE

Everyone has got to believe in something.

You better start with yourself

Be who you want to be.

Believe in YOU.

Believe that you are who you are.

Believe that you lived everything that you have,

And that you have so much to give.

Believe in YOU.

Believe that you CAN.

You can fulfill your dreams.

You can make the difference.

Believe that you can say the things that you want to say.

Believe that you can do the things you want to do. And that

You are doing them. Day after day, as you get to the bigger

Picture and you realize how much you actually have done.

Believe in You.

Believe in the people around you. What affect can you have on Them?

Believe in you.

Believe in your children, your offspring.

Believe in your friends. Believe in your family.

If I write to you from my soul, I feel love. I feel loved.

I am loved. I am pure Love.

And SO ARE YOU

There is Evil in us. It is constantly working within. Our fight is to push against all Evil.

We can do it. We are doing it. This is it. Today. You're Day. The Chance to Believe. Believe in yourself when you praise. And make it happen. Demons telling you things. Things you don't want to hear. Hurtful words resonate in your ears. And you don't want to hear. Go away. It only hurts. You want me to be in more pain in sorrow. But I will stay away. I will surround myself with goodness, with prayers of gratitude for my strength, prayers of gratitude for my bravery for the chance to live the life I want to right now. I am grateful for the lessons I have learned for the people I have met. Each encounter is a life learning lesson. And we surrender with energy for we all need each other.

And so, for me everything takes a long time to soak in; to process, and to help me evolve and to finally come to conclusion and transcend.

And today I write

I write for the good

I write for those who need to be heard to share to support TO BE AND TO LIVE life freely

Because the truth will set you free (someone once told me)

And yes, it is true

Say the truth that is what I intend to always do

Life is beautiful but I did not always see it that way

My little young eyes could not see life always beautiful, that little girl sometimes saw darkness and her mind wondered through the whole world, but she always saw with heart and soul through LOVE. Pure True Love, luckily for her, that is what her parents and siblings had taught her and fostered in her. That is the LEGACY she would like to leave.

To love yourself you also need to be in control of yourself. Be Responsible for your own actions, your thoughts, your emotions. You need to know who you are. And who you are is not defined by your job position, your family hierarchy, the color of your skin or who your friends are, or whether you have or not have a partner.

I had a need to learn who I am and where I was going. Me, not my mother, not my sister, not my friends, but ME. And so, to find my path did not come easily, not at all. And today I am still working on that path. Because who we are today is not who we are tomorrow because our experiences mold us, teach us and make us wiser.

Imagine if we stay satisfied with who we are today we would stagnate, that is why we continue to ask the questions. And as we do, we are constantly evolving and becoming a better version of ourselves.

< ....(What is the purpose you will give to your life. Are you going to live for a higher purpose while here? I want the satisfaction of being and feeling alive. And even if I am not certain of what I want in life, I am learning what I don't want to see. I don't want to see women being abused, I don't want to see a world of injustice, I don't want to see hungry mistreated children, or an elderly being taken advantage. I don't want to see people taking advantage of others. I want to see a world of justice, a world of respect a world of harmony. Stop for a minute, look in front of the mirror, see you, really see you, see inside of you..........

LETTER TO MY SISTER AND BROTHERS SEEING YOU WITHIN TRANSFORMATION

And I say

As I feel

For my daughter

For my children

I see her

Innocent

And it hurts

And I lack the STRENGTH

And it is hard so very hard

It is rough it is tough

Imagine.

And I STOP.

And I WAIT

And I remember

I don't forget

And I sigh

I am in PAIN it really HURTS

And I am about to SCREAM

I Will explode

So, I ask for HELP

In GOD I Trust

And I lean

I remember

Once Again

I breath one more time Again and again

And I leave

For a moment

I look back

But this time I do it differently in a different way

From another side

It is looking inside, but from the outside

That is, it. What my angels taught me

Look within but from the outside. You are on stage.

You are your own Director

No judgement. Nothing is good. Nothing is bad

Things just are the way they should be at this moment

And you take those hands Nearly hands

They extend to you

And they lift you up

You embrace all those who are supportive and take them with

You

We are one

You hear that

But do you understand that

Do you even feel it?

We are somehow all connected, and we feel each other's hurt

And as we feel the pain, we heal each other

We heal ourselves and we heal the pain for ourselves

I am formally trained in Vocational Rehabilitation Counselling, Addiction Specialty and Holistic Nutrition to Manage Administrate and Sales Department of a Boutique Hotel Business. I drew from all types of Social Service knowledge to completely manage a Hotel Business. Times were rough. As you know business has its ups and downs. After my father past, the main companies that used the Business services at the Hotel went bankrupt and disappeared because they were producing ZERO, others, were producing much less, and our business future was uncertain. That hit the hotel business hard, as it did many other businesses of course. Our production line was going down as well. This prompted my brothers to make a change in our business to create a TEAM with the vision that together we could do better with a shared Mission.

Even though I can honestly say it was not my area of expertise neither my career background nor my interest (Business), through the bumps, ups and downs, I definitely learned so much about managing a business as I learned about Managing Life Itself. The stress is not worth it. What is worth much is the Experience of learning that TODAY you do the best you can. Focus on one task at a time so you can complete it successfully. Believe in Yourself. Trust Life Itself. Prioritize. Be yourself, no matter how professional you may be, ALWAYS BE YOU, genuine, Your Authentic Self. That will mark the difference in everything you do.

< …. (CHANGE…… change the pattern change the habit change the thought in order to change.

It doesn't have to stay that way. If you recognize it, change it, change what you don't like. Make it better. Make it Shine. Make it Bright.)…..<

Leaving the Past Living Today. Beginning

Live the life you want to live

How do I do that I ask

When you only know to fly with one just one wing

I have learned to do that

Fly with just one wing

I see left I see right I see black I see white

I see high I see down

278

I feel weak I keep strong

I do well I come down

I think good I turn around

I see bad I go inside

The deeper I dig the farther away I become

The more I begin the closer to the end it feels

Where am I, I ask

I try to touch a solid base a new beginning maybe something

outside

But no answer seems right

Keep going you will know

Keep trying it will come

Don't stop

Never give up

This is it

Today you tried.

Do I understand

Do I know

Do I believe

Do I feel

Do I say

Do I go, do I stay?

What should I do?

What my heart tells

It is confusing yes, it is

Nothing makes sense to me

I still live

I get up I pick up I move on

I believe

There is a place

There is a time

Now is LIVE life as it comes

Now is hear your inner voice

Follow your gut

Push yourself

Keep on going

Try harder

It is today your day

Tomorrow something else will come

And what does not make any sense to you

Tomorrow it will all be clear to your eyes.

I intend to leave a legacy that all your dreams may come true if you DO something about them. And so why not mine? Yesterday I dreamt with living closer to nature and today I have the opportunity right in front of me. Visualize, that is what I learned.

Visualize all that you want for yourself. Today I can see myself opening the door of my new B & B welcoming, with a big smile on my lips, each one of my guests one by one making them feel so welcome, so pampered, so loved, at home! So, stay tuned for the next Entrepreneur Adventure coming in Peru!

About Viviana Malamud

Viviana Malamud is an International Bestseller, Hotelier, Certified Genotype Change Coach and Entrepreneur with advanced degrees in human science (psychology, vocational counseling and holistic nutrition) and a passion to be a lifelong learner. Through her vast scope of expertise, she has had opportunity to learn about people, herself and healing not within the physical or emotional realm, but to wholeness. Her life experiences have led way to mantras such as; NOT GIVING UP; NOT STOPPING, PERSEVERING, Elevating Consciousness, and to choose a path of Love. She is an analogical poet with beliefs that we all need help from others and that we need to help others along the path of illumination. It is her belief that we must have "angels" along the way to remind us to wake up and keep following our path.

Choose your path, FOCUS and Follow it. Be true to yourself. Accept Yourself, Believe in Yourself. Choose. We are free to make choices. Be Responsible for your own actions and choices. Risk. Be Authentic. And to Love Yourself, Allow for the following:

Yourself to think and observe those thoughts first.

Risk and pay for the price.

Look for whatever you think you need.

And allow yourself to feel whatever it is you feel not what others think you feel.

And finally, to be whoever it is you are not what others want you to become.

Be Free to Be that person you want to be.

You can connect with me through our website at www.DanielsApartHotel.com

Lima Peru

EPILOGUE

Life is a journey of experiences that lead to potential epiphany, through tough and sometimes difficult seasons of learning. However, ultimately it is through this process of refinement and perseverance that we become enlightened to the undeniable Truth. The truth that pain is universal and unavoidable, but that it equips us to develop resiliency skills for the life purpose we were ordained to live out for the good of all humanity.

Unstoppable did not only share the unique experiences of all the contributing authors, but equally important the content illuminated Light into the darkness, instilled hope to the wavering, and offered strategies and solutions to navigate some of life's most difficult occurrences.

"Life has a funny way of seeking to disrupt our organized system...to redirect us towards His mission for our lives... **(Dede Lomenick).**

"The ability to dream and imagine cannot be taken away and it is always available no matter the circumstance... **(Anastasia Pitanova).**

"You will hear a whisper that will tug you to surrender...than anticipate abundance realized **(Mary Jane Piedra).**

*"We have to feel the pain, allow it to surface, try to address it, but don't ignore it or sweep it under the rug...create your new normal... **(Cristina Conte Lopez)**.*

*"The greatest healing power there is, is Love... **(Julietta Wenzel)**.*

*"You never know how strong you are, until being strong is the only choice... **(Miranda Parma-Vera)**.*

*"To embrace something new you must be willing to let go of the old... **(Nadine Raphael)**.*

*"To properly heal, you have to feel your feelings and then let them go... **(Kim Andy)**.*

*"Sometimes your walk into darkness leads you to your purpose... **(Karen Prescod)**.*

*"Some circumstances leave you with the reality that there is only room for faith and belief in something bigger than yourself... **(Nancy Beer)**.*

*"Sometimes you have to realize that you are not sad for what you had and lost, but rather you are sad for what you thought you had and didn't...forgive yourself... **(Nicole Harvick)**.*

*"There is significance and purpose to suffering and you need to learn to be a good steward of these experiences... **(Debra Marsalisi).***

*"I needed to let go to heal my soul before I could heal my body... **(Wendy Marquard-Picard).***

*"It's not how deep in the gutter you are, but the steps you take to get out and be better... **(Terry Gobanga).***

*"We are all vulnerable to the blindness that prevents us from recognizing we are wise in our own eyes and we don't know what we don't know... **(Dr. Andrea Hazim).***

*"Mountains are symbolic of life, which I believe is an uphill journey that requires effort, because we cannot coast to success... **(Ginger Martin).***

*"Seasons of brokenness that cultivated humility are the cornerstone for seasons of prosperity... **(Jacob Salem).***

*"Make the decision to live, to fight another day... **(Catrese Kilgore).***

*"Have a dream, be prepared to fight for it, do not allow yourself to be defeated and eventually you will earn your freedom... **(Sean Mullervy).***

286

*"See challenges as opportunities to grow and to become more... **(Raymond Meinhardt).***

*"There are experiences in life where we create belief systems that do not serve us...Own the concept that we are the creators of our own reality and extinguish the belief that life just happens to us... **(Dr. Elaine Cruz-Abril).***

*"The truth is that those with a calling on their life are typically unqualified, but God qualifies them for his purpose... **(Jovanna Martinez).***

*"Victories occur at the intersection of opportunity and remaining unstoppable... **(Mark Robbins).***

*"My reality is my perception of it, it is not reality. I was the problem therefore I am the solution... **(Viviana Malamud).***

Learn to leverage your internal resources, to cultivate acceptance of what is not within your control, to reframe the experience in a non-judgmental manner, to edify and equip yourself, to become all you are meant to be.

An Unstoppable Warriors!

Dr. Jessica Vera, Ph.D.

Award Winning Multiple Bestseller

Founder, Elite Foundation

Thriving-Survivor Leader: Warrior For Change

EliteFundsFreedom.org   #ItEndsWithUs   #EndHT

NOTE OF APPRECIATION

The saying, "It takes a village" could not be a more accurate description of Elite Foundation's operant philosophy. The Foundation is a 501(c)(3) nonprofit organization that stands in the gap to educate, empower and to help others evolve their full potential to become Warriors for Change. By investing in yourself in our goods and services, know that you are funding freedom for those who need our help most. All royalties from our goods and services fund lifesaving services that are part of Elite's *Pathway to Their Freedom*. For more information about our community services please visit www. EliteFundsFreedom.org

The Foundation is able to expand the work that it does with survivors of human exploitation in all its ugly forms and victims of sex trafficking, due to the generosity, integrity and commitment from all our trustees, board members, community partners, donors, volunteers and you, the socially conscious consumer.

Each of our collaborative books in our world class international bestselling series features dozens of writers, who like you had a dream to become an author, and an impactful message to share with the world. We would like to thank each contributing author for their authenticity, transparency and contribution to the literary work in Unstoppable. Each author is a **Thriving-Survivor and Warrior for Change**.

Our production services that include Indie publishing and content creation are predicated on the belief that your story matters and that storytelling is the *Key to Your Success*. If you have an interest in sharing your story, we are happy to receive a request for consideration by writing to: ElitePublisher@EliteFundsFreedom.org

Subsequent to receipt of your request for a consultation, our dedicated literary staff will contact you, provide an NDA and walk you through the next steps to becoming an author.

We would like to extend a warm Thank You of appreciation to our production team members, who specialize in working with writers, who are at different stages of the writing process. Whether you are interested in being a contributing author in one of our collaborative world class international bestselling book series, or you have a book idea, or a developed concept, we have the tailored service that will meet your need.

On behalf of Wendy Elliott, the co-founder of Elite Foundation, and myself, Dr. Jessica Vera thank you for purchasing our goods and services. Know that it takes just $4.11 a day, to set a survivor on the *Pathway to Their Freedom.*

Onward and upward Warriors!

#ENDHUMANEXPLOITATION
#ENDHUMANTRAFFICKING #ITENDSWITHUS

Made in the USA
Columbia, SC
19 June 2019